CANINE CARE & CUISINE

Also by Alexandra Bastedo and published by Robson Books

Beware Dobermans, Donkeys and Ducks

CANINE CARE
& CUISINE

THE HEALTHY DOG BOOK

ALEXANDRA BASTEDO
and
JEANNIE KEMNITZER

 Robson Books

First published in Great Britain in 1997 by Robson Books Ltd, Bolsover House, 5–6 Clipstone Street, London W1P 8LE

British Library Cataloguing in Publication Data
A catalogue record for this title is available from the British Library

ISBN 1 86105 118 2

All illustrations by Sue Martin, with additional illustrations on pp. 205, 217, 223 and 224 kindly provided by Pollyanna Pickering.

Disclaimer: The authors and publisher shall have neither liability nor responsibility for any dog or person with respect to any loss or damage caused, or alleged to be caused, directly or indirectly, by the information contained in this book. All information was correct at the time of going to press.

Typeset in 10.5/14pt Stone Serif by Columns Design Ltd., Reading. Printed in Great Britain by St Edmundsbury Press Ltd., Bury St Edmunds, Suffolk.

CONTENTS

I want my boy to have a dog,
Or maybe two or three.
He'll learn from him much easier
Than he will learn from me.
A dog will teach him how to love
And bear no grudge or hate;
I'm not so good at that myself,
But a dog will do it straight.

Traditional

PREFACE

I was always very impressed by the longevity of Alexandra Bastedo's many animals and she told me this was due to the vitamin/mineral supplements and antioxodants that her doctor had prescribed for herself but which she gave to her animals as well. She said it was a shame that more good supplements were not available for dogs and cats.

I read the extensive **Canine Care & Cuisine** book that Alexandra had written with Jeannie Kemnitzer and was happy to give it my approval, having been impressed by the way our fussy dogs and those of my parents eagerly devoured Jeannie's healthy home-made dog food.

In cooking food some of the vitamin values are lost and I recommended to Alexandra and Jeannie the addition of a selection of vitamins, minerals, antioxidants and essential oils. They in turn asked me to advise on my formulas, which I have done, and which have been used in creating the Canine Care Range. All the vitamin/mineral supplements, anti-oxidants, essential oils, and dog food recipes have been tried on patients and our dogs.

I'm looking forward to reading Alexandra and Jeannie's next book **Cat Care & Cuisine** due out in 1998.

MARK ELLIOTT BVSc VetMFHom MRCVS
Kingley Veterinary Centre, Lavant, West Sussex

INTRODUCTION

The inevitable question, 'Whatever made you write a dogs' cookbook?' keeps cropping up. Well, total coincidence. In the summer of 1993 my friends, Amanda and Robert Daws, acquired a little cross-breed puppy which they named Tippy. They spent most of the summer down on a farm near Chichester while Amanda was appearing at the Chichester Festival Theatre in *Getting Married*. Tippy spent *her* days roaming freely in the fields with the other farm dogs, so the following spring, when Tippy found herself staying with Amanda's parents, Dorothy Tutin and Derek Waring, in London, she had trouble distinguishing the freedom of the country from the confines of the city. A tempting squirrel on Putney Common was too much to resist and off shot Tippy in pursuit, heading straight towards a relatively unused road, unfortunately that day there *was* a car. The driver tried desperately to avoid hitting Tippy, but Tippy ended up in intensive care with only a twenty per cent chance of survival. After a permanent steel plate was inserted into her front leg, however, she was on the road to recovery. So what does one send a dog as a convalescent present? Home-made dog biscuits, of course! The dogs in Singleton were most obliging in sampling my various attempts at formulating a recipe that worked, and an enthusiastic thank-you letter from Tippy put the seal on **Tippy Daws Dog Biscuits**.

A year later I met Alexandra Bastedo while working for her husband, Patrick Garland, the theatre producer and writer. One couldn't live in the Chichester area without hearing about Alexandra's animal sanctuary and her love of animals particularly since *Beware Dobermanns, Donkeys and Ducks*, her first book, had just been published. What I hadn't been prepared for was Alexandra's vast knowledge of diets for animals, their nutritional needs, and various remedies (particularly homoeopathic ones) for ailing pets. Unbeknown to me she had been purchasing my **Tippy Daws Dog Biscuits** at my outlet at Pump Bottom Farm, wondering who on earth would make home-made dog biscuits!

From an early age I got a lot of pleasure out of concocting original recipes and many people have admired my ingenuity at preparing delicious food. Perhaps it's in the genes. My father was an excellent cook, declaring that 'anyone who can read can cook' but at the same time rarely followed a recipe – his motto being 'improvise with existing'! My three brothers, Luis Jr., Paul and Bryan, inherited the same flair and have become extremely creative cooks. My mother always made specially cooked meals for our dogs; hence many of the recipes that appear in this book have been handed down from generation to generation. To this day – forty years on – whenever I meet up with my school-friend, Judith Burnett, she never fails to remind and tease me that at the age of seven I used to bring a pocketful of kibble to school as a snack (charcoal flavour was my favourite...) The one drawback or advantage whichever way one looks at it, was that I could never share my treats because nobody else liked to eat dog biscuits!

Jeannie Kemnitzer

JEANNIE KEMNITZER
Singleton, West Sussex

WHAT I LOVE ABOUT MY DOG TIPPY

My dog's liquorice snout,
Her ears that flap about.
Doleful eyes that look
Into my soul
And plead or comfort
With one glance.

I walk through the door,
She greets me barking
Before starting her
Welcome home dance.

The way she takes up
Half my bed,
Yawning at full stretch.
And she brings back tennis balls
Without me saying fetch.

My squirrel chasing,
Leaping fencing,
Running through the vale.
My fearless hound,
Who with one bound
Still lives to tell the tale.

My dog, my companion,
My confidante, my friend.
I will always love you
Till the very end.

Amanda Barton-Chapple

FOREWORD

For some time I have espoused the practice of preventative medicine, both for myself and for my animals, and my thinking has also naturally turned to their nutritional requirements. A homoeopathic doctor once said to me: 'If you put the right petrol in your car it runs perfectly and if you put the right food into a person or animal they too will function properly.' Unfortunately, that still doesn't take into account the modern world of pollution, chemicals, hormones and antibiotics; so we have included a holistic section advising on antioxidants, vitamins, minerals, essential oils, homeopathy and herbs to counteract their harmful effects.

I first heard of Jeannie through her **Tippy Daws Dog Biscuits** which were being sold at Pump Bottom Farm near Chichester. They were made of Singleton stoneground wholemeal flour, bulghur wheat, oats with bran, yeast, fresh stock, dried skimmed milk, parsley, garlic and free range eggs – all thoroughly healthy ingredients which were immediately wolfed up by my three Dobermanns. The trouble was that Pump Bottom Farm soon sold out and when I went in search of the mysterious 'Jeannie', I discovered she was in fact working for my husband!

When we met we immediately found we had a lot in common including North American ancestry and a great love of animals and concern for their welfare. However, there is one particular difference – Jeannie is a superb cook (which I am not) but through my animal sanctuary of 170 animals I do know a lot about the nutritional needs of animals at different stages of their lives and through different illnesses. The majority of canned products include additives and colourants and the makers are not obliged to itemise the ingredients. If you examine the small print on the tins you will find the contents described as 'meat and animal derivatives' or 'meat and animal by-products' and sometimes even 'vegetable derivatives'. Could somebody please tell us what a vegetable derivative is?!

We believe in this modern age there is a real need for tasty nutritional food for dogs whether they are carnivore, vegetarian, vegan or macrobiotic. In *Canine Care & Cuisine* Jeannie and I offer you a broad spectrum of delicious recipes which, together with nutritional supplements designed by our vet Mark Elliott, aim to keep your pet in optimum health.

Alexandra Bastedo

ALEXANDRA BASTEDO
Almodington, West Sussex

ACKNOWLEDGEMENTS

Our particular thanks to:-

Mark Elliott, our homoeopathic vet and Nick Thompson his associate for all their advice and approval and for keeping our dogs going into their late senior citizenship.

Major Morty Turner-Cooke, retired professional gundog trainer and field trialer, for nutritional information.

The Kennel Club Library staff, especially Elaine Camroux, for being so helpful with research.

The Chichester Library staff, especially Emma Sparkes, for help with research and tracking down books.

The staff at the Hammicks Bookshop in Chichester, especially Carmen Fernandez, for her enthusiasm about our project and ordering endless books for us.

Tim Faulkner for widening our knowledge of dogs in art.

Dr Peter Ashby for initially setting up Jeannie with her computer and printer.

Sandra Walters at Moore & Tillyer for her goodwill in photocopying all the various drafts of the typescript.

All the authors and publishers connected with the literary quotes featured throughout the book.

All the charities, associations, companies, private enterprises and private individuals for allowing us to include their details in the Appropriate Addresses, Preferred Products and Notable Names.

HOLISTIC HEALING

'Our food should be our medicine – our medicine should be our food.'

Hippocrates

Canine holistic healing is the treatment of dogs with natural remedies – homoeopathy, herbs and nutrition. We advocate the use of drugs prescribed by a qualified vet when necessary, but believe that vets' bills can be kept to a minimum if the right foods are given with the correct nutrients, in combination with preventative homoeopathic and herbal remedies.

1

Several years ago, I was very fortunate to hear of George MacLeod, MRCVS, DVSM, a vet at the forefront of homoeopathic healing. On several occasions he helped my dogs when conventional veterinary medicine failed, and his dog book on homoeopathy became my canine bible.

A dog's health is immediately visible in its coat, and dandruff or a lacklustre dry coat may be indicative of incorrect proportions of protein, fat and carbohydrate in its diet and a possible vitamin deficiency. (If the dog has consistently loose stools a veterinary-recommended wormer or Juliette de Bairacli Levy's herbal wormers should be given at least twice a year as worms can affect the correct absorption of food.) A meat-only diet is deficient in phosphorus and calcium and will cause diarrhoea, fragile bones and joint problems, together with a dull coat. Dogs need protein, fat and carbohydrates the same as humans. Vitamins are also essential to maintain the health of your dog and Vitamin C supplements are always beneficial, particularly for bigger dogs. Other necessary minerals are calcium, copper, iodine, iron, magnesium, manganese, phosphorus, potassium, selenium, sodium and zinc. Salt in tiny amounts is needed to prevent water retention or dehydration, but dogs with heart disease need a particularly low-salt diet.

Homoeopathy stems from the Greek 'homo' meaning same and 'pathos' meaning suffering, i.e. like treats like. My Dobermann, Little Dorrit, developed a nasty red rash underneath after we had gone walking along the footpath through the potato fields three days after they had been sprayed. Normal vets prescribed steroids, antibiotics and various ointments which improved the condition temporarily, but it always returned. Finally I called in Nick Thompson, who works with Mark Elliott, and he made me call the farmer to find out what chemicals had been used. Fortunately, the farmer was obliging and said that it was a tin-based spray which stayed on the potato plants for three weeks. The vet asked for a sample of the spray which the farmer agreed to give him. 'That way,' said Nick, 'we can treat like with like and create a pill which may help.' My bitch had also become very allergic to wheat but fortunately a combination of diet and homoeopathy has now cured her.

Samuel Hahnemann, the founder of modern homoeopathy, said that homoeopathy was curative rather than preventative and that one had to abide by the laws of nature. Homoeopathy could not cure if the underlying cause was bad nutrition.

KEY HOMOEOPATHIC REMEDIES

The following remedies have been compiled from various sources including *Dogs and Homeopathy, The Owner's Companion* by Mark Elliot BVSc VetMFHom MRCVS and Tony Pinkus BPharm MRPharmS. They may come in pills, liquids or powders. If your dog is being awkward and you are having trouble administering the remedy, a pill popper is very effective as it shoots the pill straight down the gullet. Liquids can be administered with a small plastic syringe and powders can be put on the fold of a piece of paper and tipped down the back of the throat. Homoeopathic remedies can be purchased from a homoeopathic vet and can usually be found at most health food shops and some of the more enlightened pharmacies. Before administering any remedies to your dog, you should first consult a homoeopathic vet who will recommend the cure.

CONDITION	REMEDY
Anal Glands	Arsenicum Album 30c
	Graphites 30c
	Hepar sulph 30c
	Merc Sol 30c
	Natrum Mur 30c
	Silica 6c
Anxiety, Fear and Aggression	Aconite 30c
	Anacardium 30c
	Argentum nitricum 30c
	Arsenicum Album 30c
	Belladonna 30c
	Gelsemium 30c
	Hyoscyamus 30c
	Ignatia 30c
	Lachesis 30c
	Nux vomica 30c
	Phosphorous 30c
	Pulsatilla 30c
	Staphysagria 30c
	Stramonium 30c

CONDITION	REMEDY
Bites and Stings:	
Wasp Stings	Ledum pal 6c
Bee and Nettle Stings, Hives and Rashes	Urtica Urens 6c
Bee Stings and Bites	Apis Mel 6c
Snake Bites	Hypericum 200c
Snake and Insect Bites	Echinacea 30x
Collapse, Stasis	Carbo veg 200
Constipation	Aesculus hippocastanum 30c
	Nux vom 30c
	Opium 30c
	Silica 30c
Diarrhoea	Aconite 30c
	Aloes 30c
	Argentum nitricum 30c
	Arsenicum album 30c
	China 30c
	Dulcamara 30c
	Gelsemium 30c
	Merc sol 30c
	Rhus tox 6c
	Sulphur 30c
	Veratrum album 30c
Distress	Rescue Remedy
Ear	Belladonna 30c
	Ferrum phos 30c
	Hepar sulph 6c & 30c
	Merc cor 30c
	Pulsatilla 30c
	Silica 30c
	Tellurium 6c
Fever:	Aconite 30c or 200c
Fever and Infection	Belladonna 30c
Exposure	Dulcamara 30c
E N Fevers	Ferrum phos 30c
Septicaemia	Pyrogen 1M
Gums and Teeth	Calc Fluor 30c
	Fragaria 6x
	Hepar Sulph 30c
	Merc Sol 30c
	Silica 30c

CONDITION	REMEDY
Injuries and Wounds:	
Abscesses	Hepar Sulph 6c, 30c
Fear, Sudden Infection	Aconite 30c
Fractures	Symphytum 6c
Infected Wounds	Silica 6c
Lacerations	Staphysagria 30c
Nerve Damage	Hypericum 200c
Punctured Wounds	Ledum Pal 6c
Trauma	Arnica 30c
Wound Healing	Hypericum & Calendula
Musculo-Skeletal	Arnica 30c
	Byronia 30c
	Calc Carb 30c
	Causticum 30c
	Conium 30c
	Ledum 30c
	Pulsatilla 30c
	Rhus tox 6c
	Ruta 6c
Shock	Aconite 30c or 200c
	Anica 30c or 200c
Skin	Arsenicum album 6c
	Graphites 6c
	Hepar sulph 6c
	Kali sulph 6c
	Allergens 30c
	Pulsatilla 6c
	Psorinum 200c
	Rhus tox 6c
	Sepia 6c
	Silica 6c
	Sulphur 6c
	Urtica Urens 6c
Urinary Tract	Apis 30c
	Berberis 6c
	Cantharis 30c
	Equisetum 6c
	Pulsatilla 12c
	Sasparilla
	Sepia 30c

TRUSTED TIPS

The following are a few useful tips which can improve the health of your dog with very little extra effort at all.

1. Bonemeal containing phosphorus and calcium can be added to meat diets if dogs are not being given marrow bones.

2. If you can, keep a patch in the garden to grow garlic and borage. The leaves are favourites with Daisy, Little Dorrit and Roscoe. In the winter you can give cooked garlic and borage oil to keep your dog in optimum condition.

3. Try and give liver once a week as it contains folic acid, but not too much as it can cause diarrhoea.

4. If you are feeding inexpensive canned foods, give cod liver oil twice a week and wheatgerm oil twice a week with a Vitamin C supplement daily for optimum health.

5. Look for additives, colourants, sugars and preservatives in canned foods and avoid them. Vitamin E is the best preservative. Ethoxiquin is made from rubber preservative! The manufacturers are not obliged to list the preservatives, but if you write to them they will inform you.

6. Semi-moist food contains preservatives and is full of sugar (sometimes 25 per cent).

7. If you have to give your dog 'instant' foods, cans are the best option, not cereal nuggets. However, 'by-products' or 'derivatives' are an unknown quantity, so try to choose tins with

minimal derivatives and by-products and high vitamin content. Even so, a lot of the vitamin content may be destroyed by the heat processing so a multi-mineral-vitamin complex is beneficial and you can add kelp, wheat germ, cooked oats, oatbran and Vitamin E directly on to the food.

8. A garlic clove is a healthy addition to food, but should not be given at the same meal as vitamins or minerals. It is very strong and is said to reduce their efficacity.

9. Sasparilla, urtica urens or cantharis can cure urinary infections.

10. Pregnant bitches are aided in whelping in their last two weeks of pregnancy by wild raspberry leaves.

11. Puppies whose mothers cannot feed them should be given fresh goats' milk, preferably unpasteurised. If there is a lactose intolerance, switch to dried chicken breast as soon as possible.

12. Cottage cheese is the least fatty, while sheeps' and goats' cheese are more digestible cheeses.

13. For problems with anal glands try brewing linseed tea.

14. A puppy's temperature may be 102, the normal dog's temperature is 101.4.

15. Before and after surgery give Chlorella Growth Factor or the Canine Care Anti-oxidant to boost the immune system.

16. For poisoning try giving salt water; vinegar and mustard, two to one to induce vomiting; 1 tablespoon of bicarbonate of soda to a $\frac{1}{4}$ of a cup of water, or the homoeopathic remedy arsenicum.

17. For arthritis give comfrey.

18. For insect bites rub on lemon or garlic juice, or give the homoeopathic remedy apisor urtica urens.

19. For stings rub on raw onion or garlic.

20. For canker of the ear mix one part lemon juice to three parts warm water or one or two drops of juniper essential oil.

21. For inflamed eyes give raw cucumber juice.

22. For constipation give dried fruits: figs, dates, raisins, prunes, fresh fruits, bran and whole grain cereals.

23. For hip dysplasia give cooked porridge oats and Vitamins C and E.

24. Honey and ginger is good for travel sickness. The homoeopathic remedies are tabacum or cocculus indicus.

25. If your dog falls into oil, it can be removed with a bath of Fairy Liquid, but keep it out of the eyes.

26. For kidney problems give couch grass and parsley.

27. Vaccinations are an object of dispute. They can harm and they can kill. Make sure your animal is in optimum condition before vaccinating. Kipling, Alexandra's Dobermann, was extremely ill after a booster vaccination and died prematurely at the age of six.

28. To keep the immune system up in these days of chemicals and pesticides, give a multi-vitamin-mineral complex regularly and extra Vitamin C, E and cod liver oil at the first sign of any trouble.

29. If your dog has a persistent cough and lung problems which may be due to a faulty heart, Mark Elliott advocates his cactus crataegus remedy. Conventional drugs may be necessary. The homoeopathic remedy rumex crispus may help coughs.

30. If you have the time and inclination, ground eggshell powder sprinkled on your dog's food is a good source of natural cal-

cium to aid bone-building. It's essential you use fresh eggs when making eggshell powder.

31. Evening primrose oil is particularly good for aches and keeping everything supple. The homoeopathic remedies ledum, rhus tox or ruta are good for stiff joints.

32. **Fleas** – *an adult flea can lay as many as 500 eggs in its lifetime.* One of Britain's top holistic veterinary experts, Timothy Couzens BVetMed VetMFHom MRCVS, recommended (in the April 1997 edition of *Pet Dogs*) the following treatments for trying to control the 'flea war':

    Dried lavender, rosemary and sage placed in dishes around the house or in muslin bags inside your dog's bed to keep fleas at bay.

    Lavender oil combed through your dog's coat as fleas won't like it.

    A daily teaspoon of organic apple cider vinegar in your dog's water bowl. (This can also help in preventing intestinal worms.)

    Vitamin Bs, as fleas don't like them. Attack them by adding some brewer's yeast to your dog's dinner.

33. You can buy herbal flea collars or you can make your own cotton collars with a piece of elastic with drops of eucalyptus oil or penny royal.

34. Fleas and worms won't like it if you add a teaspoon of raw chopped garlic to your dog's food.

35. **Skin Conditions**
    Tea tree oil and aloe vera are excellent for skin problems. Internally, give Vitamin E and aloe vera.

    Witchhazel and calamine are both calming and curative for some non-nutritional skin conditions.

For mild eczema, chop up an organic carrot. Put in a blender until perfectly smooth. Place on the infected area, bandage and leave for a couple of hours. Repeat as often as required. This treatment can also be used for minor wounds, sores or insect bites.

If your dog has very dry skin try curing it with a banana or an avocado:

a) peel a banana and mash it – add $\frac{1}{4}$ teaspoon of extra virgin olive oil – comb the mashed banana through the coat at the dry patch – allow to dry and rinse off with water

b) cut an avocado in half – remove stone – scoop out the flesh and mash – rub the inside of the avocado skin on the dry patch and then comb the mashed avocado through the coat – let it dry before rinsing off with water.

Sulphur is important when dealing with mange and should be given both internally and externally. If the mange proves very stubborn Ivermectin from the vet's may be the answer.

Skin Toner: bring 20 fl oz (570ml/2 $\frac{1}{2}$ cups) water to the boil – add 1 thinly sliced lemon – allow to steep overnight – sponge the liquid on to your dog and let it dry naturally. This is a good remedy for a dog suffering from fleas or mange.

Rubbing fresh lemon juice directly on to mange-infected areas can be beneficial.

The homoeopathic remedy for sore or broken skin is calendula.

For baldness try a raw food diet and, externally, tea tree oil. You can also rub a Vitamin E capsule and honey directly on to the skin.

36. City dogs can be bathed once a month with Johnson's Baby Shampoo. Country dogs may occasionally need an anti-flea

shampoo and an anti-parasite tonic with chrysanthemum and citronella by Corpore Sano.

37. For countering stress the Bach Flower Remedies are excellent, and ignatia is very good if the dog is grieving for someone in the family or another dog.

38. For stressed rescue dogs Mark Elliott BVSc VetMFHom MRCVS recommends Natrum mur for grief and Calc phos for disturbed puppies.

39. Silica is the homoeopathic remedy for forcing out thorns or splinters.

40. A small amount of chopped liquorice can help an incontinent dog. If your dog suffers from vomiting try adding a daily dose of fennel seeds to his diet. One teaspoon for a small dog, two teaspoons for a medium dog and three teaspoons for a large dog.

... everything on the earth has a purpose, every disease an herb to cure it, and every person a mission. This is the Indian theory of existence.

HEALTHY HINTS

'One dog's food is another dog's poison.'

Alexandra Bastedo

adapted from 'One man's food is another man's poison.'

Hippocrates

ANAEMIA

Anaemia predominantly results from a lack of iron and B vitamins. On a meat diet adding liver to the dog's diet is very important and on a vegetarian diet alfalfa, raspberry leaf and comfrey should be given. We recommend Feroglobin, which is a liquid iron and Vitamin B supplement.

ARTHRITIS

First put your dog on a diet to lose any excess weight. Extra calcium is important as are greenleaf, garlic and seaweed tablets and evening primrose oil. In severe cases the drug Vivitonin can help – consult your vet. The homoeopathic remedies ledum palustre or lac caninum may be good for rheumatic joints.

BAD BREATH

Bad breath is often caused by unhygienic teeth so a marrow bone or raw vegetables should be given to erode away the plaque. If you suspect the problem is intestinal, a fast is advised, followed by a fish and rice diet until the problem has gone. Charcoal biscuits in moderation can also help and we would advise a change of commercial dog food to Naturediet, Denes, Butcher's Tripe, Eukanuba or James Wellbeloved.

CANCER

The word cancer inspires fear in every heart. However, there are changes in diet and vitamin supplements that can help and, in some cases, even prolong life. Free range, raw or cooked meats (chicken, rabbit, turkey, pheasant and lamb), cooked mackerel, sardines, herring and tuna and raw organic vegetables (but not including parsnips, parsley and celery) are the best. If you prefer to cook the vegetables do so lightly to preserve their goodness. The most important anti-cancer vitamin is C in large doses (bioflavanoid – 4000 for humans, so scale down for the size of dog). Selenium is the most effective mineral, in combination with Vitamins A, C and E and can be bought in a selenium A-C-E complex (though you should still add more C). Echinacea in liquid form by Bioforce is the best anti-cancer herb.

The other important factors are no stress, so try to make sure your dog has a calm life and oxygen. Cancer hates oxygen so the more exercise and breathing in of country or sea air that your dog can get the better.

CATARACTS

Cataracts may be related to diabetes so cut back on any fatty or sweet treats and replace them with raw carrots and apples. Aloe vera juice, blackcurrant oil, beta carotene and Vitamin E all help maintain healthy eyes.

CONSTIPATION

Constipation is usually due to incorrect feeding although if this goes on for very long there may be an obstruction and a vet needs to be called. Oils are immediately helpful and on a regular basis oat bran should be added to your dog's meal. Raw meat, raw green vegetables and fresh fruit should also be given. Helpful supplements are: rhubarb tablets, zinc, Vitamins E and C and wheatgerm oil.

DIABETES

Diabetic dogs need to be kept on a very strict non-sugar diet which immediately eliminates a number of commercial dog food preparations that have sugar added. Home-cooked food is the surest way to maintain a healthy diabetic dog and two light meals a day at a regular time are preferable in order to keep the blood sugar levels on an even keel. The protein should be only from beans and vegetables and a little fish or lean meat. Chromium is the best mineral to reduce blood sugar and brown rice, oats, nuts and seeds are rich in the necessary Vitamin Bs. A limited amount of fruit should be given but Vitamin C can be added also. Herbally a dandelion root tea is beneficial along with seaweed and garlic tablets. If you suspect the diabetic condition is causing the eyesight to deteriorate extra Vitamin E and beta-carotene are important. The homoeopathic remedy natrum sulphuricum may help.

Syzigium jambolanum

This remedy can be useful in cases of diabetes and may be used in conjunction with daily insulin injections, which may be essential if you are to keep your pet well. It is quite simple to learn this technique and give the injections yourself at home once the veterinary surgeon has established the dosage. The syzigium in a suggested potency of 3× given three times daily can help to reduce the amount of insulin that has to be injected daily and in some mild cases may replace the insulin altogether.

DIARRHOEA

The absolute must with diarrhoea is a twenty-four hour fast with just water or a little lukewarm water and honey. The ideal convalescent menu is cooked diced chicken or fish mixed with white rice until the dog is back to normal. Eliminate all dairy products as this may be the cause and give boiled, bottled or filtered water in case there is a change in your water supply. When your dog is showing signs of improvement you can switch to Naturediet, Hill's Science Diet or Denes during convalescence.

The homoeopathic remedies are antimonium crudum, dulcamara, natrum sulphuricum, phosphorus or sepia.

FITS

Always seek veterinary advice. My Poodle, Noddy, had fits as a puppy. We were advised to lock him in a dark cupboard until they passed so he did himself a minimum amount of injury. They may be inherited, equally there is a theory that immunisation may be the cause. I would advise caution over vaccines for a dog who has fits, as its immune system may already be impaired. A hypo-allergenic diet should also be followed as colourants or allergies may trigger a fit. In his ninth year my Golden Retriever, Ben, developed a large lump on his head and started to have fits. We sought veterinary advice but as it proved to be a tumour and eventually the fits became intolerable for him, we had to have him put down humanely. On the occasions when I have had to have my dogs put to sleep I have always fed them their favourite chocolates. That way they hardly notice the needle going in and pass away serenely.

HEART

If your dog is obese the first thing is to reduce its weight. I always blamed myself for my Dobermann Sophie's heart condition as she had been fed far too many titbits and was definitely too fat, which put a strain on the heart. From then on she had small egg, tofu, poultry, rabbit, fish and rice meals twice daily and I would only feed her Denes tins, which they assured us did not contain salt. Omega 3 fatty acids are essential for a heart condition and can be found in mackerel, herring, sardine and tuna or given in capsule form. If you need to add bulk to the meals you can add oatbran, wheat germ and vegetables. Important supplements for the heart are: Vitamins C and E, garlic and greenleaf tablets.

HYPERTENSION

This may be due to the colourants and additives in the pet food you are feeding so read the small print and buy the more expensive brands that do not have them. Avoid raw or red meat and instead opt for cooked fish, vegetarian, vegan or macrobiotic diets. The dog may be lacking potassium and calcium so bananas, broccoli, celery, cottage cheese, goats' milk and tomatoes should be given. Chlorella is a good supplement as in Serenum (Mark & Chappell Ltd). Bach Rescue Remedy is good for immediate relief.

KIDNEYS

There are good homoeopathic remedies available for kidney infections such as cantharis which cured my thirteen-year-old Dobermann, Daisy, recently or sasaparilla. However in serious cases antibiotics may be necessary and your vet should be consulted. For an on-going problem a low protein diet is best with fish, poultry or rabbit and carrots and broccoli as the main vegetables. The dog needs to drink to flush out the kidneys and pure water, barley water and diluted cranberry juice (2/3 water to $\frac{1}{3}$ juice) are preferable. Yeast should be avoided but Vitamin C, Bs, cod liver oil and greenleaf tablets can help.

LIVER

This can be fatal and a vet should be consulted. However you can help by feeding a high fibre/low fat diet with plenty of fish, wholemeal bread and brown rice and by avoiding milk, eggs and red meat. Sesame seeds are a particularly good source of lecithin which is vital for the liver, so you can sprinkle sesame seeds or add tahini to flavour dishes. Extra bulk and fibre can be made up with oatbran or rice bran and wheatgerm. Fasting once a week can be beneficial and the only drinks should be bottled water or barley water and honey. The herbal recommendation is diced dandelion leaves mixed in with the food.

PERITONITIS

This can be a fatal condition and you should demand instant veterinary attention, as well as blood tests and X-rays. When Kipling my young Dobermann was ill the hair stood up on his back, he had an uncomfortable hunched walk, he stopped eating and, finally, I saw blood in his motions. His condition was mis-diagnosed for seven days. 'It's gastro-enteritis' was the vet's verdict one day, then 'It's an enlarged prostate'. When he died on the operating table a week later the vet said, 'If we'd got the diagnosis right on the first day, he'd still be here.' That was little comfort, so act quickly.

TATT (TIRED ALL THE TIME)

'You are what you eat.' If your dog is showing signs of lethargy make sure you are feeding good quality, nutritious food. If he's receiving commercial cans check the small print and change to a more additive-free, vitamin-rich brand. He could be suffering from a lack of folic acid, in which case add green vegetables, lentils, oats and wheatgerm to his diet or a folic acid pill. He could also receive an increase in iron from liver, kidneys, sunflower and sesame seeds and various pulses. Extra supplements that are helpful are a Vitamin B complex, Vitamin C, chlorella, kelp, beta-carotene, the herb gentian and arnica. Daisy, my thirteen year old Dobermann, is sleeping a lot more in her old age and gets most help from extra Vitamin C (1000 twice a day) and Canine Care Essential Anti-oxidants, Vitamin/Mineral Supplement and Essential Oils.

VACCINATION

Ever since my young Dobermann became very ill with a runny nose and cough after a vaccination I have been very wary of having my dogs vaccinated. It was therefore with great interest that I read Catherine O'Driscoll's book on vaccination, *Who Killed the Darling Buds of May?* According to one vaccine manufacturer only fifteen dogs in three million had adverse reactions from the doses. Catherine found out that all her six dogs had developed diseases – thyroid, arthritis, leukaemia, paralysis and death, cancer and allergies – all of which were associated by scientific heavyweights with vaccine damage. Six out of six was certainly not the odds the vaccine manufacturers had claimed.

However the vaccine manufacturers advise vets that adverse reactions might occur if:

- the dog is genetically defective
- there is something wrong with the dog's diet
- the dog was unhealthy when vaccinated
- the dog was stressed at the time of the injection
- the dog's immune system is incompetent
- the dog is exposed to the virus within a given time-frame after vaccination
- the dog is taking immune-suppressive drugs
- the vet stores and handles the vaccine inappropriately
- a puppy still has the maternal anti-body in his system, which could interfere with the effectiveness of the vaccine

According to Catherine's experience the adverse reaction may not manifest itself immediately but can appear a few months later. So beware and think carefully before you vaccinate your dog, particularly on a regular, annual basis.

If you have any doubts go to a homoeopathic vet and ask for the homoeopathic alternative. According to Richard Allport, the homoeopathic vet at the Natural Medicine Veterinary Centre: 'most veterinary surgeons in conventional practice feel that the normal vaccinations are, on the whole, safe and effective; but the majority of homoeopathic vets have serious worries about the effect of conventional vaccines on the immune system.' He adds: 'There seems a strong possibility that conventional vaccines may be a factor in the development of chronic diseases such as eczema, colitis, and auto-immune conditions.' For kennel cough, parvovirus (causes acute sickness and diarrhoea), leptospirosis (a disease of the liver and kidneys), hepatitis (a disease of the liver) and distemper (hardpad), homoeopathic nosodes (remedies made from the particular virus) are on the market.

WORMING

In her book *The Complete Herbal Handbook For The Dog And Cat* the herbalist Juliette de Bairacli Levy is adamant that chemical wormer drugs should not be used on puppies or adults. For tapeworms de Bairacli Levy recommends a day and a night of fasting followed by small round cakes containing fresh rue, wormwood and cayenne pepper (of the hottest variety). One part of the first two ingredients to two parts pepper, bound together with thick honey and flour made into a tablespoon of the mixture. This can then be pressed into small cakes and pushed down the throat. After half an hour she recommends a strong dose of castor oil or Epsom salts. She says Tabasco sauce is a safe concentration of cayenne and can be used with fifteen to twenty drops mixed into the flour and honey for an average-sized dog.

For roundworms she advocates a fast of one day for a young puppy while giving water with a little honey (one teaspoon per bowl for an average puppy) and two days for a six-month-old or adult puppy. On the night of the fast they should be given a strong does of castor oil (one dessertspoon for an average-sized puppy under six months, less for a puppy under three months) and one and a half tablespoons for an adult Cocker-sized dog, and two tablespoons for an adult Greyhound-type dog.

The following day six to eight three-grain tablets with garlic, rue or eucalyptus or other herbal worming tablets should be given. Thirty minutes later another laxative does of castor oil should be given and thirty minutes later a laxative feed in semi-liquid form of milk thickened with tree-barks' flour, honey and flaked oats.

In a dog's daily diet she suggests one or two of the following worm-removing aids at a time: grated raw coconut, grated raw carrot, ground pumpkin seeds (raw), cut seeds (raw) of nasturtium and papaya, whole grapeseeds, whole melon pips or finely chopped garlic. One teaspoon of the above for an average-sized puppy and one dessertspoon for a Cocker-sized adult, given twice daily.

Francis Hunter MRCVS VetMFHp, Homoeopathic Veterinay surgeon and acupuncturist writes:

I have to disagree with what Juliette de Bairacli Levy writes on the subject of worming in the extract above taken from *The Complete Herbal Handbook for the Dog and Cat*.

i. Roundworms: Over a period of more than 40 years in general veterinary practice I can say that worming products have improved enormously during the last 10-15 years in both efficiency and the possible adverse reaction that they might have on the animals being dosed with them. Roundworm treatments on the whole are now quite gentle in their action and are extremely effective. Worming does not have to be carried out so frequently that long-standing side effects (such as with prolonged use of antibiotic or steroids) are likely.

I feel that it is quite wrong and potentially more harmful to starve a young puppy for one or two days. I cannot agree that it is right to withhold meals from animals of any age or species. Animals live by routine and cannot understand why they are not receiving regular feeding. Moreover the thought of giving any animals castor oil appals me.

ii. Tapeworms: I do agree that tapeworms are more difficult to remove because the head has to be dislodged from the intestinal lining of the host, which calls for harsher remedies. Here again modern treatments are very effective and adverse reactions few.

Worming is important and it is my opinion that it is preferable to consult your veterinary surgeon and obtain modern treatments, rather than purchasing patent medicines over the counter.

It is interesting to note that Juliette de Bairacli Levy's book was written over 15 years ago, while Francis Hunter's comments are obviously much more recent.

(Please note that if your dog shows any signs of illness, you must first consult your vet. The above suggestions are merely 'healthy hints', to be used only in conjunction with your vet's advice after consultation.)

IF YOUR DOG...

If your dog shows signs of unusual aggression for no obvious reason, it could indicate your pet is suffering from physical pain such as arthritis.

If your dog chews its paw or mutilates itself, this may be due to lack of exercise, boredom or stress.

If your dog appears to be short of breath, or coughs, it could mean a heart problem.

If your dog's appetite alters, this could mean there is a serious problem such as kidney failure.

If the hair on your dog's back stands up, you need urgent veterinary advice.

If your dog suddenly starts to drink a large amount of water and urinates frequently, this could mean the onset of diabetes or kidney failure.

If the inside of your dog's mouth and the conjunctiva in the eye are pale, it could be a sign that your pet is suffering from anaemia.

If your dog has white faeces do not be alarmed, this could be due to eating bones.

If your dog has smelly faeces you would be advised to change its diet. The purer the food the more is used by the body and the less is excreted. This could be the answer to cleaner parks and pavements too!

If your dog has an overall bad smell, this could mean an ear infection, gum, kidney or skin problem.

... CALL YOUR VET

NUTRITIONAL NEEDS

What does a dog need? It is not a question that is easily answered, as circumstances alter cases. I remember my effete Yorkshire Terriers would only eat diced chicken in London, but the moment we took them on a walking holiday in the mountains they reverted to their true terrier selves. They were so ravenous they even begged for crusts from our sandwiches. Back in my London flat with their daily walk in Hyde Park they returned to their usual pernickety selves. The experts' views on how much protein a dog should have in its daily ration vary considerably – from 18 per cent to 40 per cent. Mark Elliott, our homoeopathic vet, advocates

40 per cent, as a general rule. However we do believe that if a dog has too much protein without enough channelled physical activity, it could lead to destructive, hyper-active and, in some breeds, even vicious behaviour.

A proper diet must include the essential elements – protein, carbohydrates, fats, vitamins and minerals – in the correct proportion. It is also important to strike the right balance between liquids and solids. This can be achieved by feeding your dog fresh home-cooked food which can often work out cheaper than purchasing commercial dog food, if you buy carefully.

> 'Extracts from the St Paul's Cathedral account book for the winter of 1666–7: "… To the Bell-ringers for feeding the Dogs that guard that Church [St Paul's] £1–6-8."'
>
> from *Plague and Fire London 1665–66*
> Leonard W. Cowie

Naturally, it won't be as cheap to feed dogs now as it was in 1666, but you will be surprised how economical it can be.

Protein is found in meat, eggs, milk, yeast and some plants. Carbohydrates are found in cereals, bread, biscuits, rice, grains and potatoes and should not exceed more that 60 per cent of a dog's diet at any one time. Fats are found in vegetable oils, meat and whole milk and should not exceed more than 5 per cent of a dog's diet. Vitamins and minerals are found in most foods such as meat, fish, milk, eggs, grains and vegetables. If you are in any doubt about the nutrition your dog is receiving you can always give it a child's multi-vitamin/mineral complex, scaled down for the size of dog, or the Canine Care Anti-oxidant and Canine Care Essential Vitamins and Canine Care Multi-Minerals.

> 'He fought with the he-dogs, and winked at the she-dogs,
> A thing that had never been *heard* of before.
> 'For the stigma of gluttony, I care not a button!' he
> Cried, and ate all he could swallow – and more.'
>
> from *The Little Dog's Day*
> by Rupert Brooke

The amount of food needed to feed a dog varies according to its breed, age, lifestyle (active or sedentary), state of health, and climate (dogs need more food in cold weather). A recent survey carried out by Hill's Pet Nutrition discovered that some of the most obese dogs in Europe live in the UK, and Lynne Hill, Veterinary Affairs Manager at Hill's, put this down to the fact that, unwittingly, ' ... owners are killing their pets with kindness, confusing overfeeding with expressing affection'. Metabolisms differ even between dogs of the same size, so it would be impossible to calculate precisely how much food to give your dog. A rough guideline would be to say one ounce (30g) of food per day for every pound of a dog's weight. For example:

Dog's Weight	Amount of Food Per Day
20 lbs (9kg)	1 lb 4 oz (570g)

A twenty-pound adult dog would need approximately 680 calories daily. The recipes in this book are based on an average-sized adult dog (e.g. an English Springer Spaniel), so you can either halve or double up on the quantities, depending on the size of your dog. At the end of the day the ideal amount of food you feed is enough to maintain an animal in optimum health.

As a dog's digestive system works on the basis of 6+ hours, whereas a human's works on 20+ hours, a dog doesn't need as many meals as we do. An average-sized dog should be served one meal a day, preferably in the morning, or 75 per cent of its meal in the morning and 25 per cent in the afternoon. Smaller breeds seem to prefer two meals a day. Most of us are brought up to feed our dogs their main meal in the late afternoon/early evening, which means they need to relieve themselves about midnight. This is rarely feasible because most people don't walk their dogs at that hour, and since they have been trained not to relieve themselves in the house a large number of pets end up at the vet's with anal problems. Avoid feeding a meal directly before or after exercise – a dog can't digest its food properly when it is tired and overheated. And talking about 'overheated', it is best to feed your dog lukewarm food – never hot and never straight from the refrigerator, i.e. room temperature (68°F or 20°C). Once you have made up any of our recipes, it is advisable to store them in the refrigerator because we do not use any preservatives. Buying and cooking in bulk and freezing the food can prove to be economical both in terms of time and money. However, on no account should you freeze any cooked fish and never freeze food more than once.

In case your dog is sensitive to aluminium, we suggest you use only cast-iron, stainless steel or ceramic pots and pans. Most non-stick pans have aluminium components and should be avoided.

Whatever you decide is best for your pet, try to keep to a routine without becoming a slave to your dog. 'Saki' warns us that if you let your dog rule your life, it could put a strain on a marriage or partnership. Mrs Strudwarden's constantly pampering her Pomeranian, Louis, led Mr Strudwarden to the following outburst:

> '"Look here," said Strudwarden, "this eternal Louis business is getting to be a ridiculous nuisance. Nothing can be done, no plans can be made, without some veto connected with that animal's whims or convenience being imposed. If you were a priest in attendance on some African fetish you couldn't set up a more elaborate code of restrictions. I believe you'd ask the Government to put off a General Election if you thought it would interfere with Louis's comfort in any way."'

from *Louis*
by 'Saki'

COMMERCIAL DOG FOOD

'Roy wanted to tell his father the truth about Space Dog, but he had to hold his tongue. He was the only one who knew that Space Dog never ate a bit of the dog food that the Barneses bought. He ate people food. Roy secretly threw the dog food away.'

from *Space Dog the Hero*
by Natalie Standiford

Most of us are guilty of leading an instant 'ready-made' life, and we have been persuaded by the Pet Food Industry through its seductive advertising to include our dogs in that 'instant' formula. How much easier to open a tin or sack of dried food than actually to spend time toiling over the oven for our precious pooches.

Since researching the available pet foods for this book with Jeannie I have found it very hard to find products that I find acceptable for my dogs. Apart from the 'with lamb' or 'with chicken' advertised in big letters on the front have you ever looked at the small print on the back? We suggest, in fairness to your dog, that you start now – and warn you that you are in for a few surprises! From October 1997 the pet food companies will be obliged to put the percentage of the meat advertised in the small print and this will have to be a minimum of four per cent. However, a tin contains 100 per cent so on the whole 96 per cent you will read contains 'animal derivatives', 'animal by-products', sometimes 'vegetable derivatives', moisture and often caramel, colourants and additives. Prior to the BSE scandal most people, like myself with my poultry, were unaware of what they were feeding their animals – namely Scrapie–infected dead sheep. We are appalled that the pet food industry, on the whole, will not let us know what we are feeding our dogs. Why not? Would we be so shocked that we would stop buying instant foods and start cooking real meat, vegetables and grains? Surely that can be the only reason. In the *Earth Island Journal* (Fall 1990 & Summer 1996), which is published in the USA, they ran articles about how euthanased dogs and cats were sent to the pet food rendering plants. There, incredibly, they were boiled up with the other miscellanea from the meat industry and put into pet foods. We do not know if this has happened in the UK, but would still be a lot happier if we were allowed to know what animal derivatives and by-products actually are.

However, we were startled to read the following excerpt taken from a piece entitled 'Pet Food theory over dog in BSE alert' which appeared in the *Daily Mail* on Tuesday, 22 April 1997:

> 'Scientists are investigating what might be the first case of mad cow disease transferring to a pet dog.
>
> A postmortem examination on an 11-year-old golden

retriever found changes in the brain which are similar to those seen in infected cows and humans.

The dog was owned by a family in Norway, where scientists believe the BSE could have come from canned food imported from the UK. Norway imports most of its dog and cat food from England. Before 1994 there was no quality control inspection.

There are question marks over the theory, however. For while more than 70 pet cats are known to have developed the disease in Britain, no dog has been diagnosed.

The pet food industry acted quickly to ensure infected material was not included in the mix after BSE was first recognised.

Manufacturers stopped using offal which included potentially infectious BSE material in April 1989.

If you look carefully you will find that some instant pet foods are better than others and we would strongly advise you to search them out. Some, like Butcher's Tripe, contain 26 per cent tripe and no additives or colourants and others, like Hill's Science Diet, have far more vitamins and minerals. Semi-moist foods often contain a lot of sugar and textured soy and dried foods also vary enormously in quality.

We have not been able to itemise all the 'small print' of the available dog foods, but we are giving you a random sampling so that you get some idea of what you are actually buying. Unfortunately you tend to get what you pay for. Puppies, pregnant bitches and dogs recovering from illness should be on a high-protein diet, so Arden Grange, Eukanuba or Nutro would be good brands to use.

When you realize that you are paying on average 45p for a tin which contains only 4 per cent of what it's advertising on the front, suddenly cooking for your dog becomes a lot more economical.

CANNED/PRE-PACKED FOOD

BUTCH RABBIT FLAVOUR

Ingredients: meat and animal derivatives, vegetable protein extract. Fish and fish derivatives and minerals. Contains EEC permitted colourants.

BUTCHER'S TRIPE MIX

Ingredients: meat and animal derivatives. (Tripe 26 per cent) Derivatives of vegetable origin.

CESAR WITH TENDER PIECES OF CHICKEN & RABBIT IN LIGHT GRAVY

Ingredients: meat and animal derivatives (min. 4 per cent chicken, min. 4 per cent rabbit), derivatives of vegetable origin, various sugars, minerals.

CHAPPIE

Ingredients: fish and fish derivatives, cereals, meat and animal derivatives, minerals. Coloured with caramel.

CHUNKY WITH RABBIT, CARROTS AND PASTA

Ingredients: meat and animal derivatives (rabbit min. 4 per cent), cereals, bakery products (pasta min. 4 per cent), vegetables (carrots min. 4 per cent), vegetable protein extracts, minerals, various sugars.

DENES CHICKEN & LIVER WITH HERBS

Ingredients: meat and animal derivatives (including chicken and liver), oatmeal, maize, rice, whole egg powder, yeast powder, seaweed extract, minerals, herbs (burdock, chickweed and nettles), vitamins.

GREENFIELDS – RABBIT

Ingredients: meat and animal derivatives, water gelling agents, contains EEC permitted preservatives.

HI LIFE SPECIAL CARE HEALTHY DIET FOR ACTIVE DOGS – CHICKEN WITH VEGETABLES & BROWN RICE

Ingredients: chicken & chicken livers (min. 50 per cent), vegetables (carrots and peas min. 5 per cent), brown rice (min. 4 per cent), vitamins, minerals.

HILL'S SCIENCE DIET CANINE MAINTENANCE – CHICKEN

Ingredients: chicken, beef, cracked pearl barley, ground maize, liver, dried whey, vegetable oil, calcium carbonate, iodized salt, choline chloride, zinc oxide, ferrous sulphate, copper sulphate, manganous oxide, sodium selenite, calcium iodate.

NATUREDIET WITH RICE, CHICKEN & CARROTS (NO ARTIFICIAL INGREDIENTS, PRESERVATIVES, COLOURS OR FLAVOURS)

Ingredients: chicken min. 55 per cent, carrots min. 8 per cent, rice min. 10 per cent, natural ground bone, seaweed extract, minerals, vitamins A, D3, E.

PAL WITH MARROW BONE JELLY WITH BEEF AND LIVER

Ingredients: meat and animal derivatives (min. 4 per cent beef, min. 4 per cent liver), derivatives of vegetable origin, minerals, various sugars.

PASCOE'S COUNTRY LAMB DINNER (FREE FROM ARTIFICIAL COLOURS, PRESERVATIVES AND FLAVOURS)

Ingredients: meat and animal derivatives (lamb min. 26 per cent), vegetables (min. 4 per cent)

PEDIGREE CHUM WITH LAMB & RICE

Ingredients: meat and animal derivatives (min. 4 per cent lamb), cereals (min. 4 per cent rice), vegetable protein extracts, derivatives of vegetable origin, minerals.

SAINSBURY'S SCOUT'S SUPREME WITH RABBIT

Ingredients: meat and animal derivatives (rabbit min. 4%), vegetable protein extract, minerals, derivatives of vegetable origin, contains EC permitted colourants.

ST MICHAEL PREMIUM TRIPE VARIETY WITH CHICKEN

Ingredients: meat and animal derivatives (tripe min. 26 per cent, chicken min. 4 per cent) and minerals.

TESCO PREMIUM WITH CHICKEN TRIPE MIX

Ingredients: meat and animal derivatives (tripe 26 per cent minimum, chicken 4 per cent minimum) and minerals.

THIS PRODUCT MAY CONTAIN BEEF AND BEEF BY-PRODUCTS SOURCED FROM THE UK.

WAITROSE SPECIAL RECIPE MADE WITH TURKEY & TUNA, EGG AND SPINACH PASTA IN TOMATO SAUCE

Ingredients: meat and animal derivatives (product contains minimum 4 per cent turkey), cereals, fish and fish derivatives (product contains minimum 4 per cent tuna), bakery products (product contains minimum 4 per cent pasta), fruit (product contains minimum 4 per cent tomato), vegetable protein extracts, minerals, derivatives of vegetable origin.

WINALOT CHOICE CUTS IN MEATY JELLY WITH CHICKEN

Ingredients: meat and animal derivatives (chicken min. 4 per cent) and minerals. Contains EEC permitted colourants.

It was interesting to note that the moisture content of the above brands ranged from 77 per cent to 85 per cent. Also note that 'rabbit flavour' is not the same as 'with rabbit'. 'With rabbit' is 4 per cent; 'rabbit flavour' is just that.

DRIED FOOD

ARDEN GRANGE PRESTIGE

Ingredients: fresh chicken, chicken meal, brewer's rice, ground corn, oat flour, beet pulp, chicken fat (preserved with mixed tocopherols), fish meal, brewer's yeast, whole dried egg, linseed, lecithin, fish oil (preserved with mixed tocopherols), minerals and vitamins.

BAKERS MINCED MORSELS REAL BEEF WITH MARROWBONE FLAVOUR

Ingredients: derivatives of vegetable origin, various sugars, meat and animal derivatives (beef 4 per cent minimum), minerals, cereals, oils and fats. Contains EC permitted antioxidants and preservatives.

BEST

Ingredients: wheat, brown rice, distillers' grains, maize protein concentrate, peas, locust beans, sugar beet, linseed, soya protein concentrate, soya oil, molasses, egg powder, carrot, sunflower seeds, peanuts, seaweed, salt, calcium carbonate, natural and nature identical flavourings.

BETA PET

Ingredients: cereals, derivatives of vegetable origin, meat and animal derivatives, oils and fats and minerals. Contains EEC permitted antioxidants and preservatives.

CHAPPIE COMPLETE ORIGINAL

Ingredients: cereals, derivatives of vegetable origin, meat and animal derivatives, oils and fats, minerals. Contains EEC permitted antioxidants and preservatives. Coloured with caramel.

ELITE REGULAR

Ingredients: poultry meat meal, ground maize, naked oats, rice flour, meat meal, animal fat, sugar beet pulp, poultry digest, dried whole egg, brewer's yeast, essential minerals and vitamins. With antioxidants butylated hydroxytoluene and butylated hydroxyanisole.

EUKANUBA PREMIUM

Ingredients: chicken meal, ground corn, chicken, rice flour, chicken fat, dried beet pulp, chicken digest, dried whole egg, fish oil, brewer's dried yeast, linseed, vitamins and minerals.

FEBO PROFESSIONAL DOG FOOD (NO ADDED COLOURS)

Ingredients: cereals, meat and animal derivatives, oils and fats, vegetable protein extracts, minerals and yeast. Contains EEC permitted antioxidants and preservatives.

GREEN ARK CEREAL MIX

Ingredients: jumbo oats, barley flakes, maize flakes, rye flakes, millet flakes, carrot powder, rubbed parsley, sunflower seeds, carob powder, coriander seed powder, dill seed powder, aniseed powder, sesame seeds, fennel seed powder.

GILPA VALU

Ingredients: Cereals, meat and animal derivatives, oils and fats, derivatives of vegetable origin, minerals and yeasts.

JAMES WELLBELOVED LAMB & RICE KIBBLE (HYPO-ALLERGENIC: NO WHEAT OR WHEAT GLUTEN, NO EGG OR DAIRY PRODUCT, NO SOYA OR CHEAP BULKING INGREDIENTS, NO ARTIFICIAL COLOURS, FLAVOURS OR PRESERVATIVES, FREE FROM GROWTH HORMONES OR DRUGS)

Ingredients: lamb meal, ground brown and pearl rice, lamb meat and bone meal, ground whole barley, lamb digest, lamb fat (preserved with natural Vitamin E and Vitamin C), linseed, alfalfa, minerals, natural seaweed, extract of yucca.

MASTERS THE COMPLETE DOG FOOD

Ingredients: cereals, meat meal, peas, linseed oil, fats and oils, minerals and vitamins. Contains: anti-oxidants BHA and BHT, colourings E110 and E124.

NUTRO'S CHOICE ADULT

Ingredients: lamb meal, ground rice, rice bran, rice flour, sunflower oil (preserved with mixed tocopherols, a source of natural Vitamin E and ascorbic acid), rice gluten, dried whole egg, natural flavours, monosodium phosphate, dried kelp (source of iodine), choline chloride, Vitamin E supplement, zinc sulfate, ascorbic acid (source of Vitamin C), niacin, ferrous sulfate, calcium pantothenate, Vitamin A supplement, manganous oxide, thiamine mononitrate (source of Vitamin B1), vitamin D3 supplement, riboflavin supplement (source of Vitamin B2), Vitamin B12 supplement, pyridoxine hydrochloride (source of Vitamin B6), inositol, folic acid, cobalt carbonate, biotin.

OSCAR SUPER PREMIUM RANGE CHICKEN & RICE (Gluten Free)

Ingredients: rice (45 per cent), chicken 35 per cent, sugar beet pulp, poultry fat, egg powder, calcium carbonate & salt.

OMEGA RECIPE COUNTRY DINNER

Ingredients: cereals, meat and animal derivatives, derivatives of vegetable origin, oils and fats, vegetable protein extracts, minerals, yeasts, vegetables. Contains EC permitted preservatives, colourants and antioxidants.

PASCOE'S ORIGINAL COMPLETE DOG FOOD WITH CHICKEN & TASTY GRAVY

(FREE FROM ARTIFICIAL COLOURS, PRESERVATIVES & FLAVOURS)
Ingredients: cereals (barley min. 4 per cent, wheat min. 4 per cent, maize min. 3 per cent), meat and animal derivatives (chicken min. 4 per cent), vegetables (peas min. 3 per cent), derivatives of vegetable origin, minerals, fish and fish derivatives. Contains EC permitted colourant: iron oxide.

PEDIGREE CHUM COMPLETE WITH CHICKEN AND RICE

Ingredients: cereals, meat and animal derivatives, derivatives of vegetable origin, oils and fats, minerals. Contains EEC permitted antioxidants, colourants and preservatives.

PEDIGREE VETERINARY PLAN 380/33

Ingredients: cereals, meat and animal derivatives, vegetable protein extracts, oils and fats, minerals, yeasts, eggs and egg derivatives.

SAINSBURY'S SCOUT'S GOURMET COMPLETE WITH LAMB, TRIPE AND VEGETABLES

Ingredients: cereals, meat and animal derivatives, derivatives of vegetable origin, oils and fats, minerals, yeast, vegetable protein extracts, vegetables. Contains EC permitted antioxidants and colourants.

WAFCOL ENERGY PLUS

Ingredients: wholewheat flour, vegetable oil, ground meat, wheat bran, soya millings, soya flour, fishmeat, glucose, calcium, yeast, vitamins and minerals.

WINALOT COMPLETE WITH BEEF & MARROWBONE WITH A RICH MEATY GRAVY COATING

Ingredients: cereals, meat and animal derivatives, vegetable protein extracts, derivatives of vegetable origin, vegetables, oils and fats, minerals and yeasts. Contains EEC permitted colourants, antioxidants and preservatives.

'Remember that junk food is not a treat: it is a slow death.'
from *You Don't Have To Feel Unwell*
by Robin Needes

A SELECTION OF AUSTRALIAN DOG FOOD

CHUM WITH BEEF (NO ADDED SALT NO PRESERVATIVES)

Ingredients: meat and meat by-products derived from beef, mutton, poultry and pork, vegetable protein, cereals, gel, food colouring, vitamin E and thiamin.

NATURE'S GIFT OATS CHICKEN AND VEGETABLES (FREE FROM ANY ARTIFICIAL ADDITIVES)

Ingredients: chicken, oats, vegetables, garlic and the necessary vitamins and minerals for maintaining health and vigour.

NATURE'S GIFT CHAR BICKIES (FREE FROM ANY ARTIFICIAL ADDITIVES)

Ingredients: flour, charcoal, fibre, molasses.

SUPERCOAT LIFE CYCLE FOOD FOR DOGS LITE – LESS ACTIVE FORMULA for older, inactive and overweight dogs (NO ARTIFICIAL COLOURS OR FLAVOURS, NO ADDED SUGAR)

Ingredients: meat and meat by-products (derived from beef and/or mutton), poultry meal, whole wheat grain, wheatgerm, rice pollard, sunflower meal, cooked cereal, vegetable oil, tallow, kelp, garlic, yeast, skim milk powder, biotin, lysine, methionine, niacin, riboflavin and all the essential vitamins, amino acids and minerals for complete dog nutrition.

A SELECTION OF CANADIAN DOG FOOD

HILL'S CANINE MAINTENANCE

On the front of the label it says TURKEY or BEEF or BEEF & CHICKEN, but if you check the small print it says 'meat by-products'. Moisture 74 per cent.

IAMS

LAMB & RICE WITHOUT BY-PRODUCTS
TURKEY WITH BY-PRODUCTS
(moisture 78 per cent)

NATURE'S CHOICE

Ingredients: lamb stock, lamb, soybean meal, ground whole brown rice, potatoes, carrots, ground whole barley, salt, Vitamin A supplement, chlorine, chloride, niacin, D3, Vitamin E, ferrous sulphate, manganous oxide, manganese sulphate, thiamin, calcium pantothenate, copper sulphate, copper prothenate, zinc oxide, zinc prothenate, cobalt carbonate, calcium iodate, riboflavin B2, B12, pyridoxine hydrochloride, folic acid, biotin.

PEDIGREE PUPPY

Ingredients: beef and poultry, meat by-products, wheat flour, wheat gluten, vitamins & minerals, caramel, water for processing.

MEATY MEALS

'He is my dog, Toto,' answered Dorothy.
'Is he made of tin, or stuffed?' asked the Lion.
'Neither. He's a-a-a meat dog,' said the girl.

from *The Wizard of Oz*
by L. Frank Baum

Dogs are predominantly carnivorous; however they can be vegetarian, vegan or macrobiotic if given a balanced diet. Equally they should never be fed an exclusively meat-only diet, as this would be nutritionally deficient. In the wild, dogs would have caught and devoured small animals, eating not just the meat but also the bones, liver, heart, kidneys etc and the grains digested by their prey. They would also have eaten available fruit and berries, grasses and trace minerals from other animals' dung.

In order for dogs to be healthy therefore, meat should not comprise more than 70 per cent of their diet. Given the worries about BSE in beef, and Scrapie in sheep, not to mention the addition of antibiotics and growth hormones, we recommend kind food meat. At the back of the book we have included the address of the Soil Association from whom you can obtain the *Soil Association Directory of Organic Farm Shops and Box Schemes*.

Obesity can be a major problem for dogs as it can lead to heart, liver, kidney, thyroid, diabetic and intestinal problems so always pick lean meat and scale down the recipe according to the size of your dog. A little oatbran and wheatgerm (vitamin B) can help provide bulk and also aid digestion (one tablespoon for the average dog).

Occasionally raw meat is very worthwhile as it makes the intestines work properly, but it should not be given to a hyperactive or aggressive dog. Marrow bones provide calcium and phosphorus, and liver is occasionally beneficial as it contains folic acid.

In catering for canines one should try and imitate nature as much as possible and rotate the menus. That way dogs get a varied, vitamin and mineral-rich diet.

If you have a word with your local butcher and tell him that you are cooking for your dog, the chances are he will be happy to let you have various off-cuts and bones at a reduced price. He may also stock frozen pet mince as do various pet shops –ox cheek, green tripe, tripe and chicken, tripe and beef, beef, chicken, lamb, turkey and rabbit.

Allen's, the butchers in Mayfair, was my Dobermann Blue's favourite shop and whenever we were in the vicinity he would drag me there on the end of his lead. He knew they were always keeping food for him and if he proferred his paw, they would give him the odd choice morsel.

RISE 'N SHINE

'A Dog starved at his Master's Gate
Predicts the ruin of the State.'

from *Auguries of Innocence*
by William Blake

3 oz (85g/1 cup) Scottish whole rolled porridge oats
10 fl oz (285ml/1 $\frac{1}{4}$ cups) boiling water
1 oz (30g) chicken livers
$\frac{1}{2}$ teaspoon extra virgin olive oil
1 teaspoon honey
1 oz (30g/$\frac{1}{3}$ cup) raisins (optional)
1 teaspoon brewer's yeast
half a kelp tablet, crushed

Pour the boiling water over the porridge oats and stir continuously
for four minutes. Meanwhile, fry the chicken livers in the olive oil
for three to four minutes. Add the honey, raisins, brewer's yeast,
kelp tablet and cooked chicken livers to the porridge oats.

If you have an egg for breakfast, crush the shell into powder
and sprinkle on top of Rise 'N Shine for added calcium.

In cold weather as an extra treat you may like to sprinkle on
a few sunflower seeds to give some added fat.

RUFUS' ROAST

Sir Winston Churchill had a Poodle called Rufus. Every evening when the family sat down to dinner, Rufus' personal cloth was put down and he was always served first.

4 oz (115g) stewing steak
2 slices (3 oz/85g) wholemeal bread
1 medium-sized carrot, sliced
1 oz (30g) onion, chopped (optional)
1 clove garlic, crushed (optional)
5 fl oz (140ml/¾ cup) Meaty Brew (page 62)

Chop up the steak, slice the bread and break into small chunks. Mix together the meat, bread, carrot, onion and garlic. Place in a greased casserole dish. Pour over Meaty Brew and bake at 350°F for 45 minutes.

Garlic improves a dog's appetite and the condition of its coat as well, as deterring worms and fleas.

DOGGIE BITES

'I loathe people who keep dogs. They are cowards who haven't got the guts to bite people themselves.'

from *A Madman's Discourse*
by August Strindberg

12 oz (340g/3 cups) organic stoneground wholemeal flour
4 oz (115g) minced lean meat (beef, chicken, turkey or lamb)
  OR 4 oz (115g) puréed cooked vegetables
  OR 4 oz (115g) Meat and Veg Pâté (page 62)
1 free range egg, beaten
1 tablespoon unrefined safflower oil
5 fl oz (140 ml/$\frac{3}{4}$ cup) Meaty Brew (page 62)

Mix the minced meat *or* puréed vegetables *or* Meat & Veg Pâté with the flour until it looks like stiff breadcrumbs. Beat together the egg and safflower oil and add to flour mixture. Add Meaty Brew to create the consistency of dough which you can then roll out on a floured board to approximately $\frac{1}{4}'$ thick. Cut with a small gingerbread man or cat-shaped cutter. Place Doggie Bites on a greased baking tray and bake at 300°F for 1 hour and 20 minutes. Allow them to cool on the tray.

Safflower oil has more linoleic acid than any other oil (up to 80 per cent) which may help to lower the cholesterol level in the blood.

LUIS' GUK

Jeannie says: 'If my father, Luis, was ever left with instructions by my mother to 'feed the dogs', this is what they got whether they liked it or not (and so did we, I seem to remember!); but judging by how Shandy and Brandy, our yellow Labrador Retriever and English Springer Spaniel, always golloped up guk, it was a firm favourite.'

4 oz (115g) lean minced beef
1 teaspoon unrefined corn oil
a pinch of chili powder or a drop of Tabasco pepper sauce (optional)
1 tin (198g) Heinz macaroni cheese
$\frac{1}{2}$ oz (15g) carrot, grated
a handful of Crunchy Crumbs (page 176)

Fry the beef in corn oil until brown. Add the chili powder or Tabasco pepper sauce and macaroni cheese. Heat to room temperature. Mix grated carrot with a handful of Crunchy Crumbs and sprinkle on top.

> Corn or maize oil is a popular cooking oil because it is light and easy to digest. Corn is a good source of phosphorus, Vitamins A, D and E and the oil contains up to 53 per cent linoleic acid. The Peruvians started pressing corn for its valuable oil thousands of years ago and vets often recommend it to be taken internally and externally for skin problems.

BEETHOVEN'S SPAGHETTI PRELUDE

Beethoven, the St Bernard featured in a popular Hollywood film, wreaked havoc in the home of the family he adopted. Many comic situations resulted of which Charlie Chaplin would no doubt have approved – he always wanted 'a dog that would be hungry enough to be funny for his feed'.

Beethoven had a bottomless pit for a stomach; hence this dish would have merely been 'starters' for Beethoven.

1 teaspoon unrefined vegetable oil
1 oz (30g) onion, chopped
$\frac{1}{2}$ clove garlic, crushed
1 bay leaf
4 oz (115g) minced beef
$\frac{1}{2}$ oz (15g) carrot, grated
$\frac{1}{2}$ oz (15g) broccoli, diced
1 tomato, peeled & chopped (2–3 oz/55–85g)
$\frac{1}{2}$ teaspoon tomato purée
3 $\frac{1}{2}$ fl oz (100ml/$\frac{1}{3}$ cup) Meaty Brew (page 62)
2 oz (55g) wholewheat spaghetti, cooked in boiling water for eight to ten minutes
$\frac{1}{2}$ teaspoon Parmesan cheese, grated (optional)

Fry the onion, garlic and bay leaf in vegetable oil for two to three minutes. Add the meat and fry for ten minutes on a low heat. Add carrot, broccoli, tomato, tomato purée and Meaty Brew. Let it boil for about five minutes while stirring constantly until the liquid has reduced – remove the bay leaf. Mix in the wholewheat spaghetti and sprinkle on Parmesan cheese.

Bay leaves are reputed to cure everything!

SHARIK'S BREAD PUDDING

In 1849 the Russian novelist Fyodor Dostoevsky was arrested for his anti-establishment views and sent to a hard-labour camp in Siberia. In his memoirs *House of the Dead* he describes Sharik, the mongrel prison dog who lived on scraps from the kitchen and odd pieces of bread which the prisoners fed him. During Dostoevsky's incarceration Sharik became his sole beloved friend.

This meal would have been a real treat for Sharik.

2 oz (55g) stale (not mildewed) wholemeal bread
1 teaspoon unrefined sesame oil
1 oz (30g) onion, chopped
½ clove garlic, crushed
1 oz (30g) carrot, sliced
4 oz (115g) liver, chopped
2 oz (55g/¾ cup) porridge oats, uncooked
1 free range egg, beaten
5 fl oz (140ml/¾ cup) Meaty Brew (page 62)

Soak the bread in enough cold water to cover it for 20 minutes. Squeeze out all the water. Fry the onion, garlic and carrot in sesame oil for five minutes. Add the liver and fry for eight minutes. Mix together the bread, oats and egg and combine with the liver, onion, garlic and Meaty Brew. Put mixture in a greased casserole dish and bake for 40 minutes at 400°F.

Sesame oil is much sought after for it contains sesamol, a natural antioxidant, which helps to keep the oil from going rancid; hence its popularity in hot climates. Sesame oil has a high content of unsaturated fatty acids and a substantial amount of lecithin. People in the Far East and Africa have been cooking with it for centuries – it is often referred to as gingelly oil or benne oil.

STROMBOLI
STROGANOFF

'Roberto [Rossellini] gave me a dog, a little black bulldog. That was all I needed! I put him down on the black lava sand, and he disappeared; he matched the sand so closely you couldn't see him. Dear little Stromboli – what else could we call him? – stayed with me for years afterwards and barked at all the photographers.'

from *Ingrid Bergman: My Story*
by Ingrid Bergman and Alan Burgess

1 oz (30g) onion, chopped
1 oz (30g) bell pepper, chopped
$\frac{1}{2}$ oz (15g) tomato, chopped
1 teaspoon unrefined groundnut oil
4 oz (115g) stir-fry steak, cut into strips
2 tablespoons Greek-style yogurt
$\frac{1}{4}$ banana, sliced
2 oz (55g/$\frac{1}{3}$ cup) brown rice, cooked in boiling water for
    30–35 minutes

Fry the onion, pepper and tomato in groundnut oil for about three minutes. Add the steak and cook for ten minutes, occasionally turning the meat. Add the yogurt and banana. Serve on brown rice.

It is only during the last twenty years that groundnut oil has become one of the most-used oils due mainly to the discovery of its valuable vitamins, minerals and amino acids. It also has a high content of oleic acid. It is the best oil to use if your dog has diabetes. Groundnut oil is also called arachis oil.

TARTAR TARTARE

' … Tartar: he lay crouched at her feet, his fore-paws stretched out, his tail still in threatening agitation, his nostrils snorting, his bulldog eyes conscious of a dull fire. He was an honest, phlegmatic, stupid, but stubborn canine character: he loved his mistress, and John – the man who fed him – but was mostly indifferent to the rest of the world: quiet enough he was, unless struck or threatened with a stick, and that put a demon into him at once.'

from *Shirley*
by Charlotte Brontë

4 oz (115g) minced lamb
1 tablespoon parsley, chopped
1 tablespoon onion, chopped
$\frac{1}{2}$ oz (15g) raw spinach, finely chopped
1 free range egg yolk
$\frac{1}{4}$ teaspoon sesame seeds
5 oz (140g) rye bread with sunflower seeds, cut into small cubes
1 teaspoon flax-seed oil

Mix all the ingredients together.

Flax-seed oil is good for the normal functioning of all cells, tissues and organs. It is one of the richest sources of alpha-linoleic acid and aka omega–3.

BEAGLE BAKE

'The shepherd-dog comes to the house every day for some meat, and as soon as it is given him, he skulks away as if ashamed of himself.'

from *The Voyage of a Naturalist*
by Charles Darwin

2 oz (55g) lamb
2 oz (55g) liver
a pinch of oregano, chopped
1 oz (30g) broccoli florets, chopped
3 oz (85g/1 cup) oatmeal, uncooked
1 oz (30g) turnip, peeled and chopped
1 free range egg
2 fl oz (55ml/$\frac{1}{3}$ cup) Meaty Brew (page 62)

Chop the lamb and liver. Mix all the ingredients together. Bake covered in the oven at 300°F for one hour. Add more Meaty Brew if it starts to look too dry.

Although liver is rich in vitamins and minerals, avoid feeding it to your dog more than twice a week. Always make sure it comes from a reliable, healthy source – this organ stores pollutants and is the first to become diseased when an animal's health deteriorates.

Oregano aids digestion and can relieve rheumatism. It also helps to stimulate appetite and is on the whole a good tonic.

MUTZ MUTTON MUSH

' ... Mutz is learning to obey the word of command with a piece of bread upon his nose until permission is accorded to eat it – he has stolen some more legs of mutton – and I detected him myself in the street the other day investigating a barrel of tripe ... '

To John Cam Hobhouse, 19 December 1816
from *'So Late into the Night'*
Byron's Letters and Journals Volume 5, 1816–1817
edited by Leslie A. Marchand

4 oz (115g) lamb
3 oz (85g) potato
1 oz (30g) onion
$\frac{1}{2}$ carrot
$\frac{1}{2}$ leek
5 fl oz (140ml/$\frac{3}{4}$ cup) water
a pinch of garlic salt

Cut up the meat, potato, onion, carrot and leek and put in a pot with the water. Add garlic salt. Cover, bring to the boil and simmer for one hour.

HOT FLUSH CHICKEN

Elizabeth Barrett Browning retrieved her beloved Spaniel called Flush from the hands of the dog-snatchers by paying an exorbitant ransom. Her maid recalls that:

'Flush was thereafter spoiled even more than usual for at least a week. If the mistress's dog wished to have finely chopped breast of chicken with just a touch of cayenne pepper on it then, why, she would chop it and pepper it and serve it to His Lordship.'

from *Lady's Maid*
by Margaret Forster

4 oz (115g) free range chicken breast
$\frac{1}{2}$ teaspoon cornflour
a pinch of cayenne pepper
1 $\frac{1}{2}$ fl oz (40ml) V8 juice
1 fl oz (30ml) pineapple juice
1 fl oz (30ml) Meaty Brew (page 62)
$\frac{1}{2}$ oz (15g) onion, chopped
2 oz (55g/$\frac{1}{3}$ cup) brown rice, cooked in boiling water for 30–35 minutes
or 5 oz (140g) mashed potato
1 oz (30g) Brussels sprouts, cooked and chopped

Cut the chicken into bite-sized pieces (use chicken bones to make Meaty Brew) and toss in the cornflour mixed with cayenne pepper. Place in a casserole dish. Heat up V8 juice, pineapple juice, Meaty Brew and onion in a saucepan. Bring to the boil and pour over the chicken. Cook covered in the oven at 300°F for 75 minutes. Mix with brown rice or mashed potato and Brussels sprouts.

MILD FLUSH CHICKEN

2 chicken drumsticks
2 pints water
1 teaspoon Marmite or (Vegemite, Vitamite or Yeast Extract)
3 oz (85g/½ cup) brown rice, uncooked
4 oz (115g) fresh corn or tinned sweetcorn (no sugar or salt added)
1 tablespoon cottage cheese

Put the chicken, water and Marmite in saucepan. Bring to the boil. Simmer for 25 minutes. Add brown rice. Return to the boil. Simmer for a further 35 minutes. Drain (save liquid for making dog biscuits or flavouring a dry meal). Add the corn and cottage cheese. This recipe makes enough for two to three meals, depending on the size of your dog.

CHARLEY'S RABBIT CASSEROLES

'Sir,' I said, 'this is an unique dog. He does not live by tooth or fang. He respects the right of cats to be cats although he doesn't admire them. He turns his steps rather than disturb an earnest caterpillar. His greatest fear is that someone will point out a rabbit and suggest that he chase it. This is a dog of peace and tranquility. I suggest that the greatest danger to your bears will be pique at being ignored by Charley.'

from *Travels with Charley*
by John Steinbeck

1 teaspoon unrefined groundnut oil
1 oz (30g) onion, chopped
1 oz (30g) carrot, grated
4 oz (115g) minced rabbit
3 oz (85g/$\frac{1}{2}$ cup) brown rice, uncooked
13 fl oz (370ml) V8 juice

Sauté the onion, carrot and rabbit in the groundnut oil. Cook for six to eight minutes, stirring occasionally. Toss in the brown rice. Add V8 juice. Pour the mixture into a casserole dish and bake uncovered at 350°F for 1 $\frac{1}{2}$ hours.

1 rabbit, jointed

10 small button onions, skinned

2 tablespoons extra virgin olive oil

1 oz (30g) wholemeal flour

20 fl oz (570ml/2 $\frac{1}{2}$ cups) Meaty Brew (chicken) (page 62)

2 oz (55g) fresh egg noodles, cooked in boiling water for three to five minutes

Fry the onions in the olive oil for five minutes. Put into a casserole dish. Toss the rabbit joints in wholemeal flour and fry in the pan for 15 minutes. Add to the onions. Boil up the Meaty Brew and pour over the rabbit. Cover and bake in the oven for 2 hours at 325°F. When it has cooled, remove the flesh from bones. Serve with egg noodles.

JIP CHOP

Charles Dickens had a great love of dogs, hence their appearance in many of his novels. His daughter, Mamie, had a little mongrel called Gipsy, so it is no surprise that this name cropped up in *David Copperfield*. Dora, David Copperfield's 'child bride' had a beloved little Spaniel always referred to as Jip.

'Don't talk about being poor, and working hard!' said Dora, nestling closer to me. 'Oh, don't, don't!'
　　'My dearest love,' said I, 'the crust well-earned –'
　　'Oh, yes; but I don't want to hear any more about crusts!' said Dora. 'And Jip must have a mutton-chop every day at twelve, or he'll die.'

from *David Copperfield*
by Charles Dickens

4 oz (115g) lamb
1 teaspoon oatbran and wheatgerm
a pinch of rosemary, chopped
2 teaspoons unrefined sunflower oil
1 oz (30g) cabbage, finely chopped
2 oz (55g/$\frac{1}{3}$ cup) brown rice, cooked in boiling water for 30–35 minutes

Cut up the lamb into bite-sized chunks. Toss in oatbran and wheatgerm and rosemary. Fry in sunflower oil for ten minutes. Add the cabbage and cook for two to three minutes. Mix with brown rice.

Rosemary helps to improve digestion and circulation.

GAME KEEPER'S PILAFF PREY

Emily Brontë had a Mastiff called Keeper on whom Charlotte Brontë based Tartar in her novel Shirley. Keeper never left Emily's side and 'he walked first among the mourners to her funeral' in 1848.

4 oz (115g) duck or chicken off the bone, minced or cut into small pieces
1 teaspoon unrefined safflower oil
a pinch of marjoram, chopped
2 teaspoon natural yogurt
1 oz (30g) seedless white grapes, chopped
2 oz (55g/$\frac{1}{3}$ cup) brown rice, cooked in boiling water for 30–35 minutes
1 oz (30g) peas, cooked

Fry the duck or chicken, sprinkled with marjoram, in safflower oil for 10–12 minutes on a low heat, stirring occasionally. Add the yogurt and grapes. Mix with brown rice and peas.

Marjoram acts internally as an antiseptic and is especially good for dealing with digestive problems. Externally, marjoram can help ease rheumatism if made into a hot compress and placed on aching muscles.

RAQ OF PHEASANT

Terry Waite, one of the Beruit hostages, tells us in his book *Footfalls in Memory* that he named his Springer Spaniel 'Raq' after G. Bramwell Evens' faithful dog of the same name. Evens was known as 'Romany of the BBC', being a true gypsy, and he introduced many young listeners to the wonderful yet simple joys of nature through his programmes on *Children's Hour*. There is a special memorial to Raq in Wilmslow, Cheshire, alongside Evens' caravan.

1 pheasant
1 onion
2 cloves garlic, peeled

Skin the pheasant. Put in a casserole dish with the onion (no need to peel) and cloves of garlic. Cover with water. Put in the oven and bake for two hours at 325°F. Remove the flesh from the bones and serve with any left-over cooked vegetables and brown rice. Use some of the stock to moisten the rice.

LIVER FOR A SAGE SEALYHAM

Captain John Edwards of Sealyham had the brainwave in the 1800s of combining the Bull Terrier, Corgi, Dandie Dinmont, Flanders Basset, Fox Terrier, Old English Sheepdog and West Highland Terrier hoping that the best attributes of each breed would appear in what resulted as the Sealyham Terrier!

4 oz (115g) liver
1 tablespoon wholemeal flour
$\frac{1}{2}$ teaspoon fresh sage, chopped
2 teaspoons unrefined sesame oil
1 oz (30g) onion, chopped
2 oz (55g/$\frac{1}{3}$ cup) brown rice, cooked in boiling water for 30–35 minutes
$\frac{1}{2}$ oz (15g) carrot, grated

Cut the liver into medium-sized pieces. Mix the sage with the flour and coat the liver. Fry the liver and onion in sesame oil for eight to ten minutes, occasionally stirring. Mix the liver and onion with brown rice and serve with grated raw carrot on top.

Sage is great for vitality but at the same time has a soothing effect.

MEATY BREW

'You can never scare a dog away from a greasy hide.'
'Canis a corio nunquam absterrebitur uncto.'

from *Satires* (II, v, 83)
by Quintus Horatius Flaccus Horace

16 oz (455g) any combination of beef/lamb/chicken and rabbit
   (meat, bones, gristle, offal)
40 fl oz (2 pints UK/2 $\frac{1}{2}$ pints USA) cold water
1 teaspoon Bovril (or Marmite, Yeast Extract, Vegemite, Vitamite)
$\frac{1}{2}$ teaspoon wheatgerm oil
1 carrot, sliced
$\frac{1}{2}$ onion, sliced
1 turnip, sliced

Put the meat, bones, Bovril or Marmite and wheatgerm oil in a
saucepan with cold water. Cover and bring to the boil. Simmer for
one hour, or longer if you want to have more gelatine and calcium
drawn out of the bones and meat. Add vegetables, bring to the
boil and simmer for a further 30 minutes. Strain. If the meat was
fatty, skim off the excess fat when it has cooled.

MEAT & VEG PÂTÉ

'Waste not, want not.'
Proverb

Remove the meat from the bones (discard bones). Mix the vegetables and meat together and put in the blender. Work until you
have a smooth consistency. Mix this with cooked brown rice or
wholemeal bread and you'll have another couple of meals.

SINFUL MEAL

'Fox-terriers are born with about four times as much original sin in them as other dogs are ... '

from *Three Men in a Boat*
by Jerome K. Jerome

2 oz (55g) turkey mince
4 oz (115g) fresh tomato pasta noodles, uncooked
$\frac{1}{2}$ oz (15g) leek, finely chopped
a pinch of tarragon, chopped
10 fl oz (285ml) boiling water
1 (100g) tin tuna in soya oil

Put the turkey mince, pasta noodles, leeks and tarragon in saucepan. Pour over water. Cover and bring to the boil. Simmer for five minutes. Strain. Drain and flake the tuna (2 $\frac{1}{2}$ oz/75g) and add to the mixture.

Tarragon helps digestion and, medicinally, is good for the heart and brain.

LANCASHIRE HEELER HOT POT

The Lancashire Heeler is a ancient British breed, which is slowly disappearing, with fewer being registered annually at the Kennel Club. Instead foreign look-a-likes are being imported and there is great concern about saving our living heritage. But one bit of British heritage that will never die is Lancashire Hot Pot!

2 oz (55g) lamb, chunks
2 oz (55g) kidneys, washed, white core removed, & chopped
6 oz (170g) potato, ½ sliced/½ cubed
1 oz onion, chopped
a pinch of rosemary, chopped
5 fl oz (140ml) Meaty Brew, Scap's Tea or liquid from Mild Flush Chicken (pages 62, 160, 55)
1 oz (30g) Brussels sprouts, cooked

Put the sliced potato in the bottom of a greased casserole dish. Throw in the lamb and kidneys, followed by the onions and rosemary. Sprinkle the cubed potatoes on top. Pour over liquid. Cover and cook at 350°F for 1 hour 45 minutes. Add Brussels sprouts.

WELCOME PUG PIE

George Eliot, the Victorian novelist, was given a Pug by her friend John Blackwood in 1859. This excerpt from her letter to him about the arrival of the Pug conveys her deep emotions:

'Pug is come! – come to fill up the void left by false and narrow-hearted friends. I see already that he is without envy, hatred, or malice – that he will betray no secrets, and feel neither pain at my success nor pleasure in my chagrin.'

from *Faithful to the End*
by Celia Haddon

1 $\frac{1}{2}$ teaspoons unrefined grapeseed oil
$\frac{3}{4}$ oz (25g) onion, chopped
$\frac{1}{2}$ clove garlic, crushed
1 oz (30g) cauliflower, chopped
a pinch of coriander, chopped
4 oz (115g) lamb, minced
1 tomato, peeled and chopped (2–3 oz/55–58g)
5 oz (140g) potato, peeled
1 teaspoon natural yogurt

Sauté the onion, garlic, cauliflower and coriander in the grapeseed oil for two to three minutes. Add the lamb and tomato. Cook for ten minutes, stirring occasionally. Cook the potato in boiling water until a knife passes through easily. Mash the potato with the yogurt and serve on top of the meat mixture.

Coriander has been known to cure indigestion and act as a tonic for the heart and stomach.

MARX MEAT

George Orwell, the English novelist (pseudonym of Eric Arthur Blair), had a large, unclipped Poodle called Marx. Eric Blair fought and was wounded in the Spanish Civil War and a comrade from his contingent came to visit him in England and comments on Marx as follows:

'It was a nice dog, but of course I was amused by the name, and Eric told me he liked to see how people responded to it. Some guessed that the dog was named after Karl Marx, but others said Groucho Marx, or even Marks and Spencer.'

from *George Orwell*
by Michael Shelden

4 oz (115g) chunks of any meat
1 ½ teaspoons natural wheatgerm
1 teaspoon unrefined safflower oil
6 fl oz (170ml/¾ cup) Scap's Tea (page 160)
3 oz (85g) fresh egg noodles, cooked in boiling water for three to five minutes
2 oz (55g) Brussels sprouts, cooked

Toss the meat in the wheatgerm. Fry in the safflower oil for ten minutes, adding more oil if needed. Pour in Scap's Tea. Bring to the boil. Cover frying pan and simmer for 45 minutes. Mix with the egg noodles and Brussels sprouts.

People often think safflower oil and sunflower oil are one and the same, but in fact the plants are quite different although they are both from the *compositae* family. Ancient civilisations along the Nile and in Ethiopia cultivated the safflower – a tall, thistle-like flower whose seed produces half of its own weight in oil.

INDEPENDENCE DAY DISH

Shandy and Brandy, the Kemnitzers' yellow Labrador Retriever and Springer Spaniel, had to endure six months' quarantine when they moved from the USA to England. On their first day at home they had their favourite Independence Day Dish.

7 oz (200g/1 cup) minced turkey, chicken, lamb or beef
1¼ oz (40g/½ cup) wholemeal breadcrumbs
1¼ oz (40g/½ cup) carrot, grated
a pinch of thyme, chopped
1 free range egg, beaten
4 fl oz (115ml/½ cup) Meaty Brew (page 62)
a handful of KemKibble (page 188)

Mix together all the ingredients. Put in a greased baking tin approximately 6" × 3" (15cm × 7.5cm). Bake at 350°F oven for one hour. Drop a handful of KemKibble on top.

Thyme helps to stimulate appetite and ease food digestion. It also aids breathing.

HAVE A HEART

'When the body that lived at your single will,
When the whimper of welcome is stilled (how still),
When the spirit that answered your every mood
Is gone – wherever it goes – for good,
You will discover how much you care,
And will give your heart to a dog to tear!'

from *The Power of the Dog*
by Rudyard Kipling

$\frac{1}{2}$ oz (15g) onion, chopped
$2\frac{1}{2}$ teaspoons unrefined sunflower oil
$\frac{1}{2}$ oz (15g) fresh wholemeal breadcrumbs
a pinch of sage, chopped
a pinch of lemon rind, grated
1 teaspoon free range egg, beaten
1 heart (approx. 6 oz/170g)
1 tablespoon brown rice flour
20 fl oz (570ml/$2\frac{1}{2}$ cups) Meaty Brew (chicken) (page 62)
2 oz (55g/$\frac{1}{3}$ cup) brown rice, cooked in boiling water for 30–35 minutes
1 oz (30g) carrot, grated

Fry the onion in $\frac{1}{2}$ teaspoon of sunflower oil for five minutes. Remove from the heat and stir in the breadcrumbs, sage, lemon rind and egg (enough to bind). Wash the heart in cold water. Slit down the middle and stuff with breadcrumb mixture. Secure sides. Coat the heart with brown rice flour. Heat two teaspoons of sunflower oil and brown the heart – approximately 20 minutes. Put the heart in a casserole dish. Boil up the Meaty Brew and pour over the heart. Cover and bake in the oven for two hours at 300°F. Release sides, slice and cut up the heart. Serve with brown rice and carrot.

> Sunflower oil is rich in Vitamin E and also has a certain amount of Vitamins A & D. It is often used as a diuretic, and is beneficial if your dog is suffering with a kidney complaint.

Alternatively wash a heart. Fill the cavities with a mixture of one tablespoon oatmeal and one teaspoon wheatgerm. Put in a pot. Cover with water or a mixture of water and Meaty or Veggie Brew (pages 62, 101). Bring to the boil and simmer for two hours adding more water after the first hour. Slice and cut up the heart. Serve with 1 oz (30g) raw broccoli florets, finely chopped and 5 oz (140g/1 cup) cooked macaroni.

CARL KIDNEYS I

Carl is a friendly Rottweiler known to many children in the States from the picture-books about him. Perhaps it's due to his popularity that the Rottweiler is the second most popular breed registered at the American Kennel Club!

The Rottweiler originated in Italy and was brought to Germany by the Romans. In the Middle Ages Rottweilers were used for boar hunting and later they became invaluable for driving cattle. In the 1800s from the town of Rottweil in southern Germany came the Rottweiler as we know it today. The Rottweiler's nutritional development is particularly slow and they should be fed like a puppy for 18–24 months even though they would physically appear to be fully grown at 10–12 months.

1 oz (30g) bell pepper, chopped

1 teaspoon unrefined corn oil

4 oz (115g) kidneys, washed, white core removed and chopped

1 tablespoon brown rice flour

a pinch of tarragon, chopped

1 free range egg, beaten

1 tablespoon natural wheatgerm

2 oz (55g/$\frac{1}{2}$ cup) macaroni, cooked in boiling water for 18–20 minutes

$\frac{1}{4}$ apple, cored, peeled and chopped

Fry the bell pepper in corn oil. Toss the kidneys in brown rice flour mixed with tarragon. Dip the kidneys in egg and then coat with wheatgerm. Put it all in the frying pan and cook for 12 minutes. Add more oil if necessary and stir frequently. Mix with macaroni and apple.

CARL KIDNEYS II

4 oz (115g) kidneys, washed and white core removed
1 oz (30g) carrot, sliced
$\frac{1}{2}$ stick of celery, sliced
1 oz (30g) turnip, peeled and chopped
1 oz (30g) cauliflower floret, chopped
a pinch of basil, chopped
$2\frac{1}{2}$ pints water
2 oz (55g/$\frac{1}{2}$ cup) macaroni, cooked in boiling water for 18–20 minutes

Soak the kidneys in cold water for 30 minutes. Drain. Chop the kidneys. Put all the ingredients except the macaroni in a large saucepan. Bring it to the boil. If there is any scum, spoon it off. Simmer for $1\frac{1}{2}$ hours uncovered, or until the water has almost totally reduced. Mix in macaroni.

Basil is good for nerves and the digestive system. It is rich in minerals and contains Vitamin B.

BOATSWAIN'S LAMB IN BLANKET

Lord Byron's Newfoundland called Boatswain died on 18 November 1808, and Byron had a monument built in the garden of the family home at Newstead Abbey in honour of Boatswain. Byron's tribute to his dog shows the deep admiration and devotion he had for Boatswain:

'Near this spot
Are deposited the Remains
of one
Who possessed Beauty
Without Vanity,
Strength without Insolence,
Courage without Ferocity,
And all the Virtues of Man
Without his Vices.'

1 medium-sized potato
1 lamb sausage flavoured with rosemary
1 oz (30g) courgette, grated
1 oz (30g) carrot, grated

Make a hole through the centre of the potato with an apple corer. Insert the sausage in the hole and bake the potato in its jacket in the oven for $1\frac{1}{2}$ hours at 400°F. Allow to cool and cut into bite-sized pieces for your dog and mix with the courgette and carrot.

BOBBY'S HOTCH POTCH

In 1858 John Gray died and was buried in Old Greyfriar's graveyard in Edinburgh. For fourteen years his devoted Skye Terrier, Bobby, stayed by the gravestone day and night, which earned him the name of 'Greyfriar's Bobby'. The gravediggers managed to coax him with milk and treats, but Bobby eventually got to know Sergeant Scott's lunch time and with military precision met him daily at George IV Bridge, shared a meal with him, and then returned faithfully to his master's grave.

1 lamb shank
1 teaspoon extra virgin olive oil
$\frac{1}{2}$ oz (15g) onion, chopped
1 oz (30g) turnip, chopped
1 oz (30g) celery, chopped
20 fl oz (570ml) cold water
1 oz (30g) cauliflower florets, chopped
1 oz (30g) carrot, sliced
1 oz (30g) lettuce, shredded
1 tablespoon parsley, chopped

Fry the lamb shank in the olive oil for 10–12 minutes, turning once. Add the onion, turnip, celery and the water. Bring to the boil, cover and simmer for one hour. Add the cauliflower and carrot and simmer uncovered for 20 minutes. Take the lamb shank out and remove all the meat from the bones. Discard the bones and return the meat to the pot, along with the lettuce and parsley. Heat gently for a few minutes. Some Crunchy Chunks (page 176) would go well with this dish.

IN THE RAW

'A carnivorous animal, living on a straight meat diet, he was
in full flower, at the high tide of his life, overspilling with
vigor and virility.'

A description of 'Buck' from *The Call of the Wild*
by Jack London

When possible getting back to what nature intended seems to be
the best formula for healthy canines. Dogs fed exclusively on raw
meat in recent international trials were found to have a higher
immune system than their counterparts fed on cooked fare.

'He [Buck] could take a ptarmigan from its nest, kill a rabbit
as it slept, and snap in mid air the little chipmunks ... Fish,
in open pools, were not too quick for him; nor were beaver,
mending their dams, too wary.'

from *The Call of the Wild*
by Jack London

We have come up with a selection of raw recipes which should be
fed occasionally to your dog. Always make sure the meat is fresh
and from a reliable source. It is not advisable to serve raw meat to
a dog that shows signs of hypertension or aggression.

Chicken

Raw chicken (without bones) and wings are a firm favourite with
nearly every breed of dog. Raw chicken has less protein than beef
or lamb and has a high fatty acid content. It is rich in potassium,
low in sodium, calcium and magnesium. Minced or diced raw
chicken with oatbran and wheatgerm, flavoured with a touch of
soya sauce would make a good tasty dish.

Beef

Chopped up raw lean beef and dog biscuits moistened with Meaty Brew (page 62) make a nice crunchy meal. Raw beef is low in fat and a good source of iron and zinc. Chuck steak is particularly high in zinc, so very beneficial if your dog suffers from a skin condition or is a male with reproductive problems.

Lamb

Chunks of raw lamb served with raw shredded cabbage and oats served in Veggie Brew (page 101) makes another nourishing meal. Dr Ian Billinghurst suggests raw lamb for dogs suffering with heart or kidney problems, since it is low in sodium and high in potassium.

Liver/Kidneys/Heart

Raw liver, kidneys or heart cut into small pieces, moistened with a teaspoon of Bovril, Marmite or Vegemite and lukewarm water with the addition of some minced raw carrot or grated apple and KemKibble (page 188) is another nutritious meal.

Tripe

You should only ever serve your dog *raw* untreated tripe – the type of tripe prepared for human consumption has been scalded, scraped, cooked and bleached in edible peroxide to make it look and smell more appetising! Try mixing raw tripe with Crunchy Chunks (page 176) for a 'delectable dish of tripe'.

Anything Goes ...

Equal amounts of chunks of raw lean meat and chunks of wholemeal bread mixed together with minced or grated raw vegetables is an easy meal to prepare, full of goodness and can be varied by adding some Meaty Brew (page 62) or a raw egg.

Alternatively substitute the wholemeal bread with cooked brown rice for **Raw Risotto**!

If you were to add a teaspoon of bonemeal and a teaspoon of Canine Care Essential Oils to any of the above suggested meals, you would have the nearest to a perfect natural diet.

GIVE A DOG A BONE

'This old man, he played one,
He played nick nack on my drum;
Nick nack paddy wack give a dog a bone,
This old man came rolling home.'

from *This Old Man*
Traditional Nursery Rhyme

Dr Bruce Fogle, the London vet, recommends daily brushing of a dog's teeth with a toothbrush. However with the correct food (lacking in sugars and caramel) and an occasional bone, dogs' teeth should stay in reasonable condition all their lives.

A bone will provide the calcium, phosphorus and copper they need in their diet and the gnawing action of their teeth will remove any tartar that is building up. The Australian vet, Dr Ian

Billinghurst, recommends that you only feed your dog uncooked meaty bones, as that is what a dog would have eaten in the wild. However, we aren't sure about that. In nature dogs would have spent their day stalking and hunting their prey and fighting off other packs of dogs that strayed on to their territory. It would have been a very different existence from our domestic dogs today who, if they are lucky, are confined to a garden with one walk a day. Too much protein can make a dog hyper-active, which is not what is needed in a quiet domestic situation.

My dogs get a marrow bone or shank bone twice or three times a week. These are the only bones that you can depend on not to splinter. Sophie, the Dobermann, once removed three pheasant carcasses from the saucepan on top of the cooker and survived to tell the tale. Other people's dogs have stolen poultry and ended up with splinters of bone in the intestines and expensive vets' bills for their owners.

If you have more than one dog you should remove the bones when they have lost interest, as they attract flies and can often provide an excuse for a squabble!

A shank bone can be given a new lease of life if you fill the hole with dog biscuits which they can spend several happy hours trying to get at.

Some vets recommend feeding your dog only water and a bone every ten days, as a fast which will cleanse the system. I've tried that with my dogs but it doesn't seem to work – they still seem to expect their main meal as well, although I can get away with down-sizing the portion!

'He tried to attract the attention of the dog by calling softly to it, and when the pomeranian came up to him he shook a finger at it. The pomeranian growled. Gurov again shook a finger at it.

The woman looked up at him and immediately lowered her eyes.

"He doesn't bite," she said and blushed.

"May I give him a bone?" he asked, and when she nodded, he said amiably: "Have you been long in Yalta?"

from *Lady With Lapdog*
by Anton Chekhov

FISH FODDER

'As I was sayin', Henry, we've got six dogs. I took six fish out of the bag. I gave one fish to each dog, an', Henry, I was one fish short.'

'You counted wrong.'

from *White Fang*
by Jack London

Fish is not the natural food of dogs although Portuguese Water Spaniels, Newfoundlands, Huskies and Finnish Spitz would no doubt be given a fair amount of fish in their diets.

All fish are suitable for invalid diets, steamed or baked and served with rice, and are a good source of protein, magnesium, iodine and selenium. However, mackerel, herring, sardine and tuna are the best to serve as they have high levels of fatty acids which help to maintain a glossy coat. These fish preserve their goodness in tins with brine and can be given as an occasional (if expensive) treat. Coley is usually the cheapest fresh or frozen fish available. It is imperative to remove all the bones from fish. (Of course you could avoid bones by serving your dog squid, which in fact contains more protein than beef!) Another economical solution would be to buy minced cod, which can be found at some fish shops and is free from bones. Raw fish contains an enzyme called thiaminase, which destroys Vitamin B1; however cooking fish kills off the thiaminase enzyme. Cooked fish should never be reheated, although it can be stored in a refrigerator for up to twenty-four hours.

SCIPIO PAELLA

'Scipio: It was just in the same way that I got into the house of the masters I served. It seems that we read men's thoughts.'

Miguel de Cervantes
from *Exemplary Novels*, 'Dialogue Between Two Dogs'
trans. Walter Kelly

$\frac{1}{2}$ oz (15g) bell pepper, chopped
$\frac{1}{2}$ oz (15g) onion, chopped
$\frac{1}{2}$ clove garlic, crushed
$\frac{1}{2}$ teaspoon unrefined sunflower oil
2 oz (55g/$\frac{1}{3}$ cup) brown rice, uncooked
1 oz (30g) peas, fresh or frozen
1 tomato, peeled and chopped
2 oz (55g) coley
2 oz (55g) whiting or cod
10 fl oz (285ml/1 $\frac{1}{4}$ cups) Fish Brew (page 93)

Fry the bell pepper, onion and garlic in sunflower oil for five minutes. Add the rice, peas, tomato, fish and Fish Brew. Bring to the boil. Cover and simmer for 30 minutes. Let the paella cool before extracting the fish – skin, flake and remove any bones. Return the fish to the mixture. (If you have any left-over cooked chicken, chop it up and add to the paella.)

If you take a taste of Scipio Paella, it's more than likely you will find yourself sharing this meal with your dog, in fact, it would be rude not to!

BOUBOULE BOUILLABAISSE

In 1897 Henri de Toulouse-Lautrec sketched a Bulldog called Bouboule which belonged to Mme Palmyre, who ran a lesbian restaurant called La Souris in Paris. Both dog and owner were known to have barks worse than their bites and the French nickname 'Bouboule' suited them both – meaning having a pudgy face and physique. However one thing they didn't have in common was Bouboule's dislike of women. It is said that he used to sneak under the tables and pee on the ladies' dresses!

$\frac{1}{2}$ teaspoon extra virgin olive oil
1 oz (30g) onion, chopped
$\frac{1}{2}$ clove garlic, crushed
1 tomato (3 oz/85g), peeled and chopped
$\frac{1}{2}$ oz (15g) watercress, chopped
10 fl oz (285ml/1 $\frac{1}{4}$ cups) water
2 oz (55g) cod fillet
2 oz (55g) haddock fillet
3 oz Crunchy Chunks (page 176)
1 oz (30g) Cheddar cheese, grated (optional)

Heat the olive oil in a pan. Add onion and garlic. Fry gently for five minutes. Stir in the tomato and watercress. Pour in the water and bring to the boil. Add the fish – flesh face-down, skin on top. Cover and simmer for 25 minutes. Lift the fish out. Skin, flake and discard any bones before returning the fish to the pan. Add Crunchy Chunks and Cheddar cheese.

Extra virgin olive oil contains the least amount of impurities of any oil because olives are easy to press and the oil can be obtained without heat or chemicals. Although low in linoleic acid, olive oil is high in oleic acid (80 per cent), making it one of the most digestible of edible oils. It is also a good source of calcium and iron and helps in the absorption of the fat-soluble vitamins – A, D, E, and K.

Hippocrates declared olive oil both a food and a medicine and to the Hebrews the olive was a symbol of prosperity.

KEDGEREE FOR PICKLES

Pickles, a Terrier, appears in Beatrix Potter's *The Tale of Ginger and Pickles*. Pickles and Ginger, a yellow tomcat, ran the village shop. They let all their customers have their groceries on credit and because of this there was hardly any money and they were obliged to eat their own goods. One day there wasn't enough money to pay for Pickles' dog licence or the rates and taxes. So, they closed the shop and Pickles became a gamekeeper!

4 oz (115g) smoked haddock
1 free range egg
1 oz (30g) cauliflower florets, broken up
2 oz (55g/⅓ cup) brown rice, cooked in boiling water for 30–35 minutes
1 teaspoon parsley, chopped

Put the smoked haddock, egg (uncracked) and cauliflower in a pan. Cover with water. Bring to the boil. Simmer for ten minutes. Drain. Skin and flake the fish – removing any bones. Peel the egg and chop. Add the fish, egg, cauliflower and parsley to brown rice.

TIMMY'S TUNA TIMBALE

' ... Timothy looks very fat and well, George dear.'
'Oh Mother, he's had a marvellous time at school,' said George. 'He really has. He chewed up the cook's old slippers ... '
'And he chased the cat that lives in the stables every time he saw her,' said Anne.
'And he once got into the larder and ate a whole steak pie,' said George; 'and once ... '

from *Five Go Adventuring Again*
by Enid Blyton

3 oz (85g/$\frac{1}{2}$ cup) macaroni, uncooked
1 stick of celery (55g/2oz), chopped
1 free range egg
2 $\frac{1}{2}$ (70g) tuna in sunflower oil, drained
a pinch of chives, chopped
$\frac{3}{4}$ oz (25g) Crunchy Chunks (page 176)
$\frac{1}{2}$ oz (15g) banana, peeled and sliced (optional)

Put the macaroni in a pot. Cover with water. Bring to the boil. After boiling for ten minutes, add the celery and egg (uncracked). Boil for another ten minutes. Drain. Peel and chop the egg. Add the tuna and chives. Top with Crunchy Chunks and banana.

Chives contain oils, iron and some sulphur and therefore help to improve appetite.

FISH ON FRIDAY

Jeannie says: 'It's strange what one remembers from one's childhood, but one thing that sticks in my mind is 'fish on Friday'. My mother was a great traditionalist and not even the dogs were let off the hook!'

4 oz (115g) cod, whiting or coley
1 free range egg
$\frac{1}{2}$ oz (15g) raw spinach, finely chopped
Crunchy Crumbs (page 176)

Place the fish in a pot. Cover with cold water. Bring to the boil. Simmer for ten minutes. Drain. Flake and remove any bones. Mix in the raw egg and spinach. Top with Crunchy Crumbs.

There are conflicting views about whether to give dogs raw or cooked eggs. In their natural environment dogs would have eaten them raw and the Kemnitzer dogs never showed any ill effects from having raw egg mixed in with their Fish On Friday. It has been said that raw egg white contains an enzyme which destroys biotin, and if fed over a long period, this can result in a biotin deficiency, causing dry hair and flaky skin. However, it is fairly unlikely that one would feed a dog sufficiently large amounts of raw egg for this to occur.

OLD MOURNFUL'S
PUB GRUB
MONDAY

' ... I did have two regular companions during my stay in Fittleworth. One was a terrier mongrel, a skinny, wiry old thing with rusty tearmarks on his cheeks and a permanently dejected manner, who adopted me as a friend. Each day when lunch was over and I came through the darkened bar into the protestant hush of the afternoon, Old Mournful would be sitting there on the forecourt, his pink tongue beating in the heat, waiting, and when I walked past he would slowly rise and wander after me, like a guardian with a melancholy duty to perform.'

from *Waiting*
by Hugo Donnelly

2 free range eggs, beaten
4 fl oz (115ml) goats' milk
1 tin (115g) Glenryck Pacific Pilchards in tomato sauce
3 oz (85g) wholemeal bread, sliced and cubed
a pinch of dill, chopped
2 oz (55g) Cheddar cheese, grated (optional)
$1\frac{1}{2}$ oz (45g) courgettes, sliced

Mix together the eggs, goats' milk, pilchards in tomato sauce, wholemeal bread, dill and Cheddar cheese. Line the base of a casserole dish with courgettes. Pour in the egg mixture. Bake at 350°F for one hour.

Dill helps the brain and the digestive system as well as giving vitality. It is also good for relieving flatulence and colic.

OLD MOURNFUL'S PUB GRUB
TUESDAY

5 oz (140g) potato, cubed
1 oz (30g) swede, peeled and sliced
1 oz (30g) carrot, peeled and sliced
4 oz (115g) cod fillet
1 teaspoon natural yogurt
$\frac{1}{4}$ teaspoon sesame seeds (optional)

Put the potato, swede and carrot in a pot. Cover with water. Bring to the boil and simmer for 10–15 minutes until the vegetables are tender. At the same time put the cod in a separate pot of boiling water and cook for ten minutes. Drain vegetables and mash with yogurt. Drain, flake and de-bone the fish and add to the vegetable mash. Sprinkle the sesame seeds on top.

> Sesame seeds are rich in vitamins and minerals – calcium, iron and protein. The god Yama in Hindu mythology blessed the sesame seed and in the East it is revered as a symbol of immortality.

OLD MOURNFUL'S PUB GRUB
WEDNESDAY

4 oz (115g) whiting
10–15 oz (285ml-430ml) Fish Brew (page 93)
$\frac{1}{2}$ oz (15g) watercress, finely chopped
1 oz (30g) broccoli florets, finely chopped
1 oz (30g) toasted oatbran

Place the whiting in a casserole dish. Pour over enough Fish Brew to cover the fish. Cover and bake in the oven for 25 minutes at 350°F. Allow to cool before skinning, flaking and de-boning. Meanwhile soak the watercress and broccoli in the hot Fish Brew for ten minutes. Drain. Mix the fish, watercress and broccoli together. Top with toasted oatbran.

OLD MOURNFUL'S PUB GRUB
THURSDAY

3 oz (85g) brown rice flakes
8 fl oz (230ml) Fish Brew (page 93)
4 oz (115g) haddock fillet
a pinch of tarragon, chopped
1 oz (30g) carrot, grated

Soak brown rice flakes in Fish Brew for 30 minutes. Gently grill the haddock for ten minutes – skin down. Turn over, remove skin and grill for a further five minutes. Allow to cool. Remove any bones and flake. Add tarragon, brown rice flakes and carrot.

OLD MOURNFUL'S PUB GRUB
FRIDAY

4 oz (115g/½ cup) broth mix – pearl barley, haricot beans, yellow split peas, green split peas, dried peas, split red lentils, brown long grain rice (yields 7 oz/200g when cooked)
2 ½ oz (70g) tuna in brine, drained
1 oz (30g) Crunchy Chunks (page 176)

Soak the broth mix in cold water for seven to ten hours. Drain. Boil in fresh water for ten minutes. Drain. Add the tuna and top with Crunchy Chunks.

> Lentils which are seeds that have been dried, dehusked and sometimes split are rich in protein. If you want to give your dog less protein we suggest you halve the broth mix and treble up on Crunchy Chunks.

FISH BREW

'Damned neuters in their middle way of steering,
Are neither fish nor flesh nor good red-herring.'
Epilogue to *The Duke of Guise*
by John Dryden

16 oz (1 lb) (455g) fish (heads, tails, skin and bones)
$1\frac{1}{4}$ litres cold water
1 carrot, chopped
1 onion, chopped
1 turnip, peeled and chopped
1 stick of celery, sliced

Put the fish in a saucepan. Add the cold water. Bring to the boil and add the vegetables. Cover and simmer for 45 minutes – any longer and it will start to taste bitter. Strain the brew through a fine sieve.

MAIDA'S MACKEREL MASH

Washington Irving, the American essayist, describes setting off for a walk with Sir Walter Scott and his dogs in 1817:

'There was the old staghound, Maida, a noble animal, and Hamlet, the black greyhound, a wild, thoughtless youngster, not yet arrived at the years of discretion; and Finette, a beautiful setter, with soft, silken hair, long pendant ears, and a mild eye, the parlour favourite. When in front of the house, we were joined by a superannuated greyhound, who came from the kitchen wagging his tail ... '

from *Faithful to the End*
by Celia Haddon

3 oz (85g) smoked mackerel fillets *or* sardines
2 tablespoons cottage cheese
2 teaspoons natural yogurt
1 teaspoon lemon juice
2 teaspoons parsley, chopped
1 oz (30g) sweetcorn
2oz (55g/$\frac{1}{3}$ cup) brown rice, cooked in boiling water for 30–35 minutes

Skin and flake the mackerel. Mix together the fish, cottage cheese, yogurt, lemon juice, sweetcorn and parsley, followed by the rice.

This is a good mash for older dogs whose teeth aren't quite as sharp as they used to be. Mackerel helps to keep a dog's coat in good condition.

Parsley is rich in Vitamin C and iron. It aids digestion and is known to be helpful to dogs suffering with rheumatism or kidney problems.

INDEPENDENCE DAY FISH

If your dog has been in kennels this makes a good easy-to-digest, welcome-home meal.

7 oz (200g) coley, whiting or cod, either separately or in a mixture
1 $\frac{1}{2}$ oz (45g) fresh breadcrumbs using brown bread with malted grains
$\frac{1}{2}$ oz (15g) leek, finely sliced
1 oz (30g) broccoli, chopped
a pinch of garlic granules
1 free range egg
4 fl oz (115ml/$\frac{1}{2}$ cup) Fish Brew (page 93)
a handful of Crunchy Crumbs (page 176)

Place the fish in a saucepan. Cover with water. Bring to the boil and simmer for ten minutes. Let it cool before skinning, flaking and removing all bones. Mix all the ingredients together except the Crunchy Crumbs. Put the mixture in a greased baking tin approximately 6" × 3" (15cm × 7.5cm) and bake at 350°F oven for one hour. Drop a handful of Crunchy Crumbs on top.

'TO HELL WITH COST'

(attributed to Samuel Goldwyn)

'She was certain these ownerless dogs would be famished. Out here, two miles or more from St Maurice, even a hunting dog would have a hard time of it. These were guard dogs, bred for aggression, not survival. Or pets that had outgrown their charm, or were costing too much to feed.'

from *Black Dogs*
by Ian McEwan

3 oz (85g) pink salmon, mashed
1 teaspoon parsley, chopped
2 oz (55g/1/3 cup) brown rice, cooked in boiling water for
    30-35 minutes
$\frac{1}{2}$ avocado, peeled and cut up into medium-sized pieces
$\frac{1}{4}$ teaspoon mugi miso, mixed with 1 tablespoon hot water
1 oz (30g) Crunchy Crumbs (page 176)

Mix the salmon, parsley, brown rice and avocado together. Combine the mugi miso and water and stir till blended. Pour over the salmon mix and add Crunchy Crumbs.

OR

3 oz (85g) pink salmon, mashed
1 oz (30g) fresh spinach, shredded
2 oz (55g) soba buckwheat noodles, cooked in boiling weater until
    swollen and tender

Mix all ingredients together.

VEGETARIAN VICTUALS

'The chief food of the natives of Otaheite consists of vegetables. They have no tame animals, except poultry, hogs, and dogs, and these are not numerous. Captain Cook and his associates agreed that a South Sea dog was little inferior to a British lamb, which is probably occasioned by their being kept up, and fed solely upon vegetables.'

from *The Philosophy of Natural History*
by William Smellie

Can dogs be exclusively vegetarian? The answer is 'yes'. Although they are predominantly carnivores it is possible, with the right combinations of food, to have a vegetarian dog. Some hyper-active dogs with behavioural problems can actually improve on a vegetarian diet.

All animals (except humans who persist in consuming dairy products past adolescence) are naturally weaned at an early age. Cow products often cause different allergies and diseases because of lactose intolerance and should only be given in small amounts – if at all. Goats' and sheep's milk, cheeses and yogurt are usually more easily tolerated and we recommend the use of free range eggs as their battery counterparts contain very little lecithin or methionine. We also advocate organic vegetables, and broccoli, cauliflower and cabbage stalks make excellent 'bones'. However, chemically treated raw carrots should be peeled first, but curiously my dogs showed no interest in carrots until I started to give them organic ones. There is of course no comparison in taste as they are so much sweeter.

All grated and chopped vegetables are an excellent source of roughage, but root vegetables such as turnips, swedes and potatoes should be cooked to make them more digestible.

If you are changing your dog from tins to a vegetarian diet do so slowly while the intestines get used to working properly again. An overnight change could make things a bit windy, although within a week this would stop!

Greengrocers often throw away imperfect vegetables. If you explain it's for animals you may find your local supplier is only too happy to give them to you instead of discarding them.

In order to have vegetarian dogs in optimum health one must rotate their menus. That way they receive the total range of vitamins and minerals in the correct ratios. Dr Pitcairn, the American vet, particularly advises the addition of extra Vitamins A, C, E and D in the right amounts, according to the size of your dog.

Meat contains high fat levels but even more harmful are the levels of pesticides, hormones, antibiotics and chemicals in intensely-farmed animals today. It is also very hard to obtain wild meat so having a vegetarian dog fed on organic produce along with pulses, grains, nuts, seeds and fruit is a very healthy option.

Protein ratings (out of 100g): Eggs 94; Milk 82 (pasteurised 70, UHT 20); Cheese 70–75.

BOB'S BREAKFAST

Bob was Emily Arundell's Wire-haired Fox Terrier whose ball was at the centre of a murder inquiry in Agatha Christie's mystery *Dumb Witness*.

'Bob and Spot, the butcher's dog, circled slowly round each other, hackles raised, growling gently. Spot was a stout dog of nondescript breed. He knew that he must not fight with the customers' dogs, but he permitted himself to tell them, by subtle indication, just exactly what mincemeat he would make of them were he free to do so.

Bob, a dog of spirit, replied in kind.'

from *Dumb Witness*
by Agatha Christie

1 oz (30g) barley flakes
1 oz (30g) rye flakes
1 oz (30g) brown rice flakes
1 oz (30g) porridge oats with bran
$\frac{1}{4}$ oz (10g) natural wheatgerm
1 tablespoon sunflower seeds
2 tablespoons unrefined sunflower oil
1 tablespoon clear honey

Put all the ingredients in a bowl and mix well. Spread the mixture evenly on a baking tray and bake in the oven for 45 minutes at 400°F, stirring occasionally. Transfer the golden brown flakes immediately on to a dish to cool. Serve with oat milk and sliced banana.

Oat milk is made from artesian spring water, oats and rapeseed oil. It has no added sugar, preservatives, cholesterol or lactose and, being dairy-free, is suitable for dogs on a vegetarian or vegan diet.

BEEHIVE OR BEHAVE

An apple a day keeps the vet away!

1 large cooking apple
1 tablespoon clear honey

Peel and core the apple. Cut horizontally into rings. Place on foil in grill pan. Spread half the honey on the apple rings. Cook for three minutes under a hot grill. Turn over the rings and spread with remaining honey. Grill for another three minutes. Stack the rings in the shape of a beehive. Allow to cool before serving with Bob's Breakfast (page 99). Only serve if your dog behaves!

VEGGIE BREW

3 oz (85g) carrot, sliced
3 oz (85g) leek, sliced
4 oz (115g) swede, peeled and chopped
2 oz (55g) celery, chopped
3 oz (85g) turnip, peeled and chopped
3 oz (85g) potato, cubed
a pinch of sea salt
1 teaspoon Marmite (Yeast Extract)
30 fl oz (1½ pints UK/1 ¾ pints approx. USA) cold water

Put the vegetables, sea salt and Marmite in a saucepan with the cold water. Cover and bring to the boil. Simmer for 35 minutes. Strain off the liquid – Veggie Brew. Save the vegetables for:

VEGGIE STEW

2 oz (55g/⅓ cup) brown rice, cooked in boiling water for 30–35 minutes
4 oz (115g) vegetables, cooked
½ teaspoon Parmesan cheese, grated (optional)

Mix the brown rice and vegetables together. Sprinkle Parmesan cheese on top.

VEGGIE PÂTÉ

Purée the vegetables from Veggie Brew and mix with Crunchy Chunks (page 176).

CASSIUS' FINAL TRIBUTE

Jeannie says, 'This book would not be complete without mentioning 'Cassius', the black Labrador Retriever who belonged to Paul Rogerson, the General Manager of the Chichester Festival Theatre. Cassius was a lovable, affable character, who gave everyone a warm welcome and always had time to listen to other people's problems ... I shared an office with Cassius and Paul for several years and if we had a working-lunch, Cassius showed a real partiality to cottage cheese and carrots. This recipe is a final tribute to Cassius and the Chichester Festival Theatre.'

2 oz (55g) cottage cheese
1 oz (30g) carrot, grated
1 teaspoon green nori flakes
3 oz (85g) KemKibble (page 188)

Mix all the ingredients together.

COLLIE CAULIFLOWER

1 oz (30g) onion, peeled and chopped
1½ oz (45g) celery, chopped
1 oz (30g) tomato, chopped
a pinch of mint, chopped
1 teaspoon unrefined grapeseed oil
1 tablespoon carrot, grated
2 dates, pitted and chopped
1½ oz Fusilli pasta, uncooked
4 oz (115g) cauliflower leaves and florets, chopped
1 tablespoon natural Greek-style yogurt

Sauté the onion, celery, tomato and mint in grapeseed oil for eight minutes. Add the carrot and dates. Meanwhile cook the Fusilli according to the instructions on the packet, but add the cauliflower for the last five minutes. Drain the Fusilli and cauliflower. Mix all the ingredients together, finally adding the yogurt.

PONTO'S NUTTY ROAST

Alfred Jingle, the itinerant actor in Charles Dickens' *The Pickwick Papers*, credits his dog with amazing intelligence (perhaps more than his owner ...):

"Ah, you should keep dogs – fine animals – sagacious creatures – dog of my own once – Pointer – surprising instinct – out shooting one day – entering enclosure – whistled – dogged stopped – whistled again – Ponto – no go; stock still – called him – Ponto, Ponto – wouldn't move – dog transfixed – staring at a board – looked up, saw an inscription – 'Gamekeeper has orders to shoot all dogs found in this enclosure' – wouldn't pass it – wonderful dog – valuable dog that – very."

from *The Pickwick Papers*
by Charles Dickens

$\frac{1}{2}$ clove garlic, crushed
1 oz (30g) onion, peeled and chopped
1 oz (30g) mushrooms, chopped
1 oz (30g) tomato, chopped
1 teaspoon parsley, chopped
$1\frac{1}{2}$ teaspoons extra virgin olive oil
4 oz (115g) mixed nuts* (walnuts, almonds and Brazil nuts), chopped
4 oz (115g) oatmeal with bran
1 free range egg, beaten
9 fl oz (255ml/$\frac{1}{2}$ pint approx. USA) Veggie Brew (page 101)

Fry the garlic, onion, mushrooms, tomato and parsley in olive oil for five minutes. Mix together the nuts and oatmeal. Add the vegetables, egg and Veggie Brew. Put the mixture in a small loaf tin and bake in the oven at 350°F for 35 minutes.

*You can use any mixture of nuts provided they don't include peanuts. Some dogs can have an allergic reaction to peanuts – in fact Roscoe, the Dobermann, raided the sack of birds' peanuts and ended up very poorly at the vet's.

'AS IT HAPPENS'

The following recipes can be varied depending on what vegetables and fruit you have available. You and your dog will be amazed at the different flavours that can be created 'as it happens'.

1. Finely chop up equal portions of courgette, onion, apple and cucumber plus a small amount of mint. Fry gently in extra virgin olive oil until softened. Add enough Greek-style yogurt with honey to make a smooth consistency but not too runny. Top with KemKibble or Crunchy Crumbs (pages 188, 176).

2. Fry, in a little unrefined vegetable oil, any left-over cooked vegetables you may have like potatoes, broccoli, cabbage, carrots etc. Add some chopped onion, chopped tomato and a bit of chopped parsley. Stir it all together before finally adding half a handful of grated Cheddar cheese and a couple of slices of Soda bread (yeast and sugar-free) broken into bite-sized pieces.

JASPER'S CORNY CARROTS

Jasper was the name of the Cocker Spaniel belonging to Maxim de Winter in Daphne du Maurier's novel *Rebecca*.

'Jasper lapped noisily at his drinking bowl below the stairs, the sound echoing in the great stone hall.'

from *Rebecca*
by Daphne du Maurier

3 oz (85g) carrots, grated

5 oz (140g) creamed sweetcorn

2 oz (55g/½ cup) macaroni, cooked in boiling water for 18–20 minutes.

Mix all the ingredients together and heat gently.

The Native American Indians and Mexicans worshipped corn and believed it to hold the powers of fertility. It has such a high nutritional value that they could exist solely on corn for months at a time. Corn is an excellent tonic for glandular problems as well as aiding in the growth of healthy hair and teeth. Dogs, as well as cats, like tinned sweetcorn, especially the creamed variety. Corn, like pineapple, does not lose its vitamins in the canning process.

POLYBE POTATO PIE

Polybe was a Mallorcan Hound that belonged to Gertrude Stein and Alice B Toklas, named after the articles signed 'Polybe' in *Figaro*. Polybe featured in many of Gertrude Stein's plays and he was remembered for having a passion for smelling roses!

6 oz (170g) potatoes, peeled and thinly sliced
1 oz (30g) carrot, grated
1 oz (30g) onion, peeled and chopped
1 free range egg, beaten
10 fl oz (285ml) Veggie Brew (page 101)

Mix the carrot and onion together. Layer, alternately, the potato slices and the carrot/onion mixture in a small loaf tin starting and finishing with the potato. Add the egg to the Veggie Brew and pour over the vegetables. Bake covered in the oven at 400°F for one hour.

MOPSER MOUSSAKA

"Has anybody seen my Mopser?
- A comely dog is he,
With hair the colour of Charles the Fifth,
And teeth like ships at sea."

from *The Bandog*
by Walter de la Mare

1 teaspoon extra virgin olive oil
2 oz (55g) courgette, chopped
½ oz (15g) carrot, grated
½ oz (15g) onion, chopped
1 oz (30g) tomato, chopped
2 oz (55g) potato, diced and cooked
4 oz (115g/¾ cup) green lentils, cooked
1 teaspoon water
¼ teaspoon Kikkoman naturally brewed soy sauce
1 ½ oz (45g) Cheddar cheese, grated (optional)
2 oz (55g) Crunchy Chunks (page 176)

Heat the olive oil in a frying pan. Add the courgette, carrot, onion and tomato. Cook for four minutes. Add the lentils, water and soy sauce. Cover and heat gently for three minutes. Add Cheddar cheese and Crunchy Chunks. Stir until the cheese has melted.

PINPIN'S PUMPKIN PIE

Emile Zola, the French novelist, had a black Pomeranian called Sir Hector Pinpin, who couldn't live without his master. In 1898, Emile Zola was sentenced to prison in connection with the Dreyfus case. However, he escaped to England for a year, but by the time he returned to Paris heralded as a hero, poor Pinpin had died from grief.

16 oz (455g) pumpkin
1 oz (30g) soy margarine
a pinch of nutmeg
1 oz (30g) Parmesan cheese, grated (optional)
1 oz (30g) fresh wholemeal breadcrumbs

Peel the pumpkin, cut in half, remove seeds and dice. Put the pumpkin pieces in a pot, cover with water and boil for 15 minutes. Drain. Melt margarine in a frying pan, add the pumpkin and nutmeg. Mix well. Place the pumpkin in a greased baking dish. Mix together the Parmesan cheese and breadcrumbs and sprinkle on top. Bake at 400°F until browned on top.

Don't throw away the pumpkin seeds if you have a bitch in season. Raw minced pumpkin seeds will do her good. In addition canned pumpkin has been known to help if your dog is suffering from constipation. It is an excellent source of fibre and by mixing a tablespoon with your dog's food for a few days you are more than likely to see an improvement.

RUMBLE-TUMS

8 oz (230g) potatoes, diced
1 ½ teaspoons unrefined sesame oil
1 oz (30g) onion, chopped
a pinch of garlic granules
3 oz (85g) cabbage, shredded
1 oz (30g) Cheddar cheese, grated (optional)

Put the potatoes in a saucepan and cover with boiling water. Cook until tender. Drain. Heat the sesame oil in a frying pan. Add onion, garlic granules and cabbage and fry for five minutes, stirring frequently. Add the potatoes and Cheddar cheese and cook for a further two minutes.

> Flatulence can be caused by too much soy or dairy products in a dog's diet. However, feeding your dog a little live yogurt has been known to improve this condition ($\frac{1}{4}$ teaspoon = small dogs; 1 teaspoon = medium-sized dogs; 1 tablespoon = large dogs).
>
> Also, you could add activated vegetable charcoal to your pet's main meal ($\frac{1}{8}$ teaspoon = small dogs; $\frac{1}{4}$ teaspoon = medium-sized dogs; $\frac{1}{2}$ teaspoon = large dogs). However, only do this for a couple of days because activated charcoal absorbs nutrients, so it could be harmful if used over a long period of time.

BROCCOLI AU BOUVIER DES FLANDRES

Bouvier des Flandres is of European origin from an area near Brussels in Belgium. This breed is believed to have descended from the griffon, a coarse-haired terrier-like dog. It was used as a cattle-droving dog until modern farming methods made it redundant. With its herding instinct the Bouvier des Flandres is great for rounding up children ...

3 oz (85g) broccoli, cooked

2 oz (55g) split peas, cooked

1 free range egg, hard-boiled

2 oz (55g) wholemeal spaghetti, cooked in boiling water with $\frac{1}{2}$ teaspoon of Marmite or Yeast Extract for eight to ten minutes

1 teaspoon sunflower seeds

Mix all the ingredients together.

SCRUMMY
FIT FOR A KING

King George VI had a Labrador Retriever called Scrummy.

2 oz (55g) Crunchy Chunks (page 176)
1 $\frac{3}{4}$ oz (50g/$\frac{1}{3}$ cup) green lentils, washed and cooked in boiling water until tender
2 $\frac{3}{4}$ oz (75g/$\frac{1}{3}$ cup) split peas, soaked in cold water for 12 hours, cooked in boiling water for ten minutes, simmered for 45–50 minutes
1 $\frac{3}{4}$ oz (50g/$\frac{1}{3}$ cup) brown rice, cooked in boiling water for 30–35 minutes
3 $\frac{1}{3}$ oz (100g/$\frac{1}{3}$ cup) cottage cheese
1 oz (30g) celery, chopped

Mix all the ingredients together.

SCRUMMY
FIT FOR A QUEEN

3 oz (85g) carrots, grated
3 oz (85g/$\frac{1}{2}$ cup) large green lentils, soaked in cold water for 12 hours, cooked in boiling water for ten minutes and simmered for 45–50 minutes
1 oz (30g) brown rice, cooked in boiling water for 30–35 minutes
1 tablespoon watercress, chopped

Mix all the ingredients together.

TAMING TABOULEH

'A hound it was, an enormous coal-black hound, but not such a hound as mortal eyes have ever seen. Fire burst from its open mouth, its eyes glowed with a smouldering glare, its muzzle and hackles and dewlap were outlined in flickering flame. Never in the delirious dream of a disordered brain could anything more savage, more appalling, more hellish, be conceived than that dark form and savage face which broke upon us out of the wall of fog.'

from *The Hound of the Baskervilles*
by Arthur Conan Doyle

A gentle meal like this could help to tame an aggressive dog!

2 oz (55g) bulghur wheat, soaked in boiling water for 30 minutes
1 tablespoon onion, chopped
1 oz (30g) cucumber, finely diced
$\frac{1}{2}$ tomato, finely chopped
1 oz (30g) bean sprouts, soaked in cold water for ten minutes
1 oz (30g) goats' cheese, crumbled
$\frac{1}{4}$ teaspoon parsley, chopped
$\frac{1}{4}$ teaspoon mint, chopped
$\frac{1}{2}$ teaspoon lemon juice

Mix all the ingredients together.

VEGAN VARIATIONS

'The act of putting into your mouth what the earth has grown is perhaps your most direct interaction with the earth.'

from *Diet For A Small Planet*
by Frances Moore Lappé

A dog can only be a healthy vegan if its owner acquires sufficient knowledge of the various pulses, grains, vegetables and fruits needed to maintain the correct nutritional balance. Vegans do not eat meat, poultry, fish, eggs or dairy products; so it is important to be aware of the protein ratings in the other foods, e.g.: (out of 100g) - Brown rice 70; Buckwheat 65; Broccoli and Brussels sprouts 60; Soy Beans 61; Lentils 30; Corn 72; Cauliflower 60; Potato 60; Oats 65; Pumpkin Seeds 60; Sesame Seeds 55; Sunflower Seeds 60; Peas 45; Chickpeas 45; Tofu 65; Walnuts 50 and Wheat 60.

The fatty acids necessary to maintain a beautiful coat come from nuts and seeds such as safflower, sunflower, corn and soy oils. Equally there is no need for a vitamin deficiency as Vitamin A is found in carrots, pumpkins, tomatoes and greens. Vitamin B is found in nuts, oats, lentils, Marmite, potatoes, dried fruit, tamari, miso, and the sea vegetables hijiki, nori and wakame. Calcium and iron are obtainable from seeds, nuts, carob, beans, tofu, parsley, sea vegetables and oatmeal.

If by any chance your dog has difficulty in tolerating bean products, alternatives to soy milk are Oat Milk or Rice Dream. Oat Milk is made from water, oats and rapeseed oil and Rice Dream contains filtered water, organic brown rice, expeller pressed high oleic safflower oil and a tiny amount of sea salt.

Fortunately most dogs like fruit, which are a valuable source of Vitamin C. My first Dobermann, Blue, would eat cherries and spit out the stones while Jeannie's Springer Spaniel, Brandy, would pick blackberries directly from the bush! All our dogs have loved apples, and I do believe that an apple a day combined with a good vitamin/mineral supplement keeps the vet away.

'6 August 1844
Here is Flush, rejoicing like Bacchus himself, among the grapes!
eating one grape after another, with exceeding complacency,
shown by swingings of the tail. 'Very good grapes, indeed!'
from *Letters of Elizabeth Barrett Browning to Mary
Russell Mitford*, edited by Meredith B Raymond and
Mary Rose Sullivan

GRUEL FOR CANDY'S DOG

'That dog of Candy's is so God damn old he can't hardly walk. Stinks like hell, too … I can smell that dog a mile away. Got no teeth, damn near blind, can't eat.'

from *Of Mice and Men*
by John Steinbeck

3 oz (85g/½ cup) organic pinhead oats
5 fl oz (140ml) freshly squeezed orange juice
5 fl oz (140ml) still spring water

Puts the oats, orange juice and water in a double boiler. Cook for 40 minutes, stirring occasionally. Leave to stand overnight. Reheat and serve with a small amount of chopped naturally dried apricots (preservative free) and alfalfa.

MUTT'S MUSHROOM MEDLEY

Mutt was the name of the charming little mongrel who was the star of Charlie Chaplin's film *A Dog's Life*.

3 oz (85g) mushrooms, chopped
$\frac{1}{2}$ oz (15g) green pepper, chopped
1 oz (30g) courgette, chopped
a pinch of thyme, chopped
1 teaspoon unrefined sunflower oil
3 oz (85g/$\frac{1}{2}$ cup) brown rice, cooked in boiling water for
    30–35 minutes
1 teaspoon walnuts, finely chopped

Sauté the mushrooms, pepper, courgette and thyme in sunflower oil for five minutes. Add brown rice and walnuts.

CAIRN CARROTS

8 oz (230g) carrots, sliced

4 fl oz (115ml/¼ pint USA) freshly squeezed orange juice

2 oz (55g/⅓ cup) brown rice, cooked in boiling water for 30–35 minutes

1 tablespoon parsley, chopped

Place the carrots in a shallow casserole dish. Pour the orange juice over the carrots – to enhance the flavour allow to stand for at least an hour, but this is not essential. Bake at 400°F, covered, for 40 minutes, stirring occasionally so that the carrots on top don't dry out. Mix with brown rice and parsley.

You can alter this recipe by substituting the orange juice with the juice of a tangarine or mandarin, which are less acidic. Surprisingly you will find that a number of dogs like orange juice; in fact we recommend occasionally placing a bowl of orange juice next to a dog's water bowl for a change.

Dogs produce their own Vitamin C, but as Diane Steen says in her book *The Natural Remedy Book for Dogs & Cats*, 'this small amount is only a fraction of the Vitamin C needed for good health, and the amount an animal's body produces may not be enough to prevent even deficiency diseases.'

Carrots are good for calming the nervous system as well as aiding digestion.

BULGHUR FOR A PIT BULL TERRIER

Can you imagine being arrested on account of your looks or ancestry, being put behind bars at a secret location, friends and relations having to pay up to £300 to visit you, having a death sentence or life imprisonment hanging over you for a crime you have never committed? It is hard to believe that this has been happening in the UK since the Dangerous Dogs Act 1991 came into force. Naturally there are some valid cases but it is the innocent victims and their owners who are suffering. So if you are a Pit Bull Terrier, Japanese Tosa, Dogo Argentino or a Fila Braziliero or a cross of these breeds, don't even think of trying to come to the UK!

4 oz (115g) tofu
$\frac{1}{4}$ teaspoon Kikkoman naturally brewed soy sauce
7 fl oz (200ml) Veggie Brew (page 101)
2 $\frac{1}{2}$ oz (70g/$\frac{1}{2}$ cup) bulghur wheat, soaked in boiling water for
    30 minutes
1 oz (30g) onion, chopped
$\frac{1}{2}$ clove garlic, crushed
4 oz (115g) carrot, sliced
1 cooking apple, peeled, cored and chopped
1 oz (30g) sultanas

Put the tofu, soy sauce and Veggie Brew in a blender and mix until smooth. Mix all the other ingredients together and add the liquid. Put in a casserole dish and bake for 40 minutes at 350°F. There should be enough for a couple of meals or more, depending on how hungry your dog is.

BOXER BALLS

2 oz (55g/⅓ cup) brown rice, cooked in boiling water for 30–35
   minutes
1 oz (30g) carrot, grated
1 oz (30g) tofu, crumbled
2 teaspoons natural wheatgerm
1 tablespoon polenta
2 teaspoons unrefined sesame oil

Blend the brown rice, tofu and carrot. Add wheatgerm. Form into
balls and roll in polenta. Fry the balls in the sesame oil for 15–20
minutes.

LAP IT UP LASSI

Lassi is a traditional Indian yogurt drink.

10 fl oz (285ml) vegan yogurt
30 fl oz (865ml) natural spring water
1 teaspoon honey

Mix the yogurt, water and honey in a blender. Work until smooth.

FANNY'S FRY-UP

In Thomas Hardy's *Far From The Madding Crowd* when Fanny is homeless and in a weakened state a 'Newfoundland, mastiff, bloodhound, or what not, it was impossible to say' befriends her and leads her to safety.

'The animal, who was as homeless as she, respectfully withdrew a step or two when the woman moved, and, seeing that she did not repulse him, he licked her hand again.'

2 teaspoons unrefined sunflower oil
4 oz (115g) tofu, crumbled
1 teaspoon parsley, chopped
2 oz (55g) cabbage, shredded
1 teaspoon watercress, chopped
$\frac{1}{4}$ teaspoon Marmite and 1 tablespoon water, boiling
1 teaspoon green nori flakes
3 oz Crunchy Chunks (page 176)

Fry the tofu, parsley, cabbage and watercress in sunflower oil for three minutes. Add Marmite and water mixed, and cook for another five minutes. Sprinkle on the nori flakes. Toss in Crunchy Chunks and mix well.

TEMPTING TOFU

2 teaspoons unrefined groundnut oil

1 oz (30g) onion, chopped

$\frac{1}{2}$ clove garlic, crushed

1 tomato, chopped

2 oz (55g) cauliflower, chopped finely

2 oz (55g) broccoli florets, chopped

1 oz (30g) courgette, sliced

a pinch of oregano, chopped

a pinch of basil, chopped

5 oz (140g) tofu, diced

1 tablespoon tomato purée

1 teaspoon clear honey

3 oz (85g) wholemeal pasta, cooked in boiling water for 15 minutes

Heat the groundnut oil and sauté all the vegetables and herbs for eight minutes. Add the tofu, tomato purée and honey. Stir well and cook for five minutes. Mix with the pasta.

SPAGHETTI ENOUGH FOR TWO

Alexandra says, 'With my Italian blood, it is not surprising that my two Dobermanns, Daisy and Little Dorrit (mother and daughter) are frequently fed spaghetti. It is amusing to watch them eat this meal because in their excitement often their bowls collide and they end up chewing on the same strand of spaghetti.'

1 oz (30g) dried soy mince, soaked in boiling water for ten minutes
1 teaspoon unrefined grapeseed oil
1 oz (30g) onion, chopped
$\frac{1}{2}$ clove garlic, crushed
1 stick of celery, chopped
2 oz (55g) mushrooms, chopped
1 teaspoon tomato purée
5 fl oz (140ml) Veggie Brew (page 101)
2 oz (55g) wholewheat spaghetti, cooked in boiling water for eight to ten minutes
1 tablespoon pine kernels, fried quickly in a little extra virgin olive oil (optional)

Fry the onion, garlic, celery and mushrooms in the grapeseed oil for three minutes. Add the soy mince, tomato purée and Veggie Brew. Cover and cook for 12 minutes. Add the spaghetti. Sprinkle on pine kernels for an added treat.

LITE LUNCHES

3 oz (85g) broccoli florets, chopped
3 oz (85g) Crunchy Crumbs (page 176)
1 teaspooon bonemeal
1 tablespoon pumpkin seeds, ground

Mix all the ingredients together.

OR

2 oz (55g) bean sprouts, soaked in cold water for ten minutes
2 oz (55g/$\frac{1}{3}$ cup) bulghur wheat, soaked in boiling water for 30 minutes
1 oz (30g) carrot, grated
1 teaspoon sunflower seeds or pine kernels, ground

Mix all the ingredients together.

OR

2 oz (55g/$\frac{1}{3}$ cup) bulghur wheat, soaked in boiling water for 30 minutes
1 oz (30g) beetroot, cooked and chopped
1 stick of celery, chopped
1 teaspoon wakame, soaked in cold water for ten minutes

Mix all the ingredients together.

BUFFY BURGERS

'Good, darling. Then I'll expect you. (*Pause*)
Yes, the dogs will be fine – yes! Yes, of course they'll be fed. (*Pause*)
Estelle! What do you think I am? I know what to feed a Gaddam Dog! (*Pause*)
Dog food, for God's sake! Any fool can feed a dog! What do you think I'm going to feed them? Chicken food? A bit of caviar and the rest of the champagne?
You're absolutely mad! I did not feed poor little Buffy alcohol! You're making a mountain over the fact that the poor thing liked a spot of brandy now and then! (*Listening*)
Esteile, the dog was not a candidate for AA, and I will not have Robert fix the dinners!'

from the play Tallulah!
by Sandra Ryan Heyward

1 oz (30g/½ cup) dried soy mince (soaked in boiling water for 10 minutes)
1 oz (30g/⅓ cup) oats with bran
1 oz (30g/⅓ cup) rye flakes
1 teaspoon green nori flakes
1 teaspoon natural wheatgerm
1 oz (30g) carrot, grated
2 tablespoons tomato juice

Squeeze out any excess water in the soy mince. Mix together well the soy mince, oats with bran, rye flakes and wheatgerm. Form into two burgers and place them on a greased baking tray. Bake in the oven at 350°F for 40 minutes, turning them over after 20 minutes. Pour the tomato juice over the burgers and serve with grated carrot.

VEGAN CRUMBLE

12 oz (340g) porridge oats with bran
6 oz self-raising wholemeal flour
1 teaspoon brewer's yeast
2 oz (55g) raisins
2 oz (55g) mixed nuts (walnuts, almonds and Brazil nuts),
  chopped
5 oz (140g) tofu, blended
6 fl oz (170g) unrefined grapeseed oil
1 tablespoon vanilla
3 oz (85g) honey

Mix the oats, flour, brewer's yeast, raisins and nuts together in a large bowl. In a smaller bowl mix the tofu, grapeseed oil, vanilla and honey. Then combine all the ingredients together in the large bowl and mix well. Spread on a greased baking tray and bake in the oven at 350°F for 20 minutes. Use sparingly as a topping.

GRAINS FOR GELERT

'Ah, what was then Llewelyn's pain,
For now the truth was clear:
His gallant hound the wolf had slain,
To save Llewelyn's heir.'

from *Beth-Gelert*
by W.R. Spencer

A Welsh legend dating back to the 13th century tells us of
Prince Llewelyn who went off to fight the English leaving his
Deerhound, Gelert, to guard his baby. When Llewelyn
returned he found his dog's mouth dripping with blood and
immediately assumed that Gelert had ravaged his son. In his
fury he plunged his sword into Gelert. Moments later he
heard the faint cries of his baby and discovered him alive
near the mangled remains of a huge wolf. Instantly Llewelyn
realized his dreadful mistake – Gelert had killed the wolf to
save his son. But it was too late. Gelert only managed to lick
his master's hand gently before expiring.

5 oz (140g) Shipton's 5 Cereals Blend – malted wheat flakes, barley
flakes, sunflower seeds, millet and oats
6 fl oz (170ml) organic apple juice

Soak the 5 Cereals Blend in the apple juice for at least 30 minutes,
or longer if your dog prefers a moister texture.

MACROBIOTIC MORSELS

'I love best to have each thing in its season only, and enjoy doing without it at all other times.'

Henry Thoreau

The macrobiotic diet has often been regarded as a fad by the Western world. However, it is a diet very much about preventative medicine, which has cured many animals of serious diseases. It is the reverse of the modern trend towards chemicals, refinement and large-scale commerce and requires a positive change in diet. Degenerative diseases such as heart disorders, cancer, arthritis, allergies and diabetes are very common today and may improve on a diet of whole grains, seeds, nuts, vegetables and fruit with meat, dairy foods and sugar being kept to a minimum. Apart from the aforementioned diseases, if a dog with hyperactive or behavioural problems is changed from canned foods to a macrobiotic diet there is usually a significant improvement in its demeanour.

Yin and Yang, the Oriental philosophy, is behind the macrobiotic diet – 'macros' in Greek meaning great and 'bios' life, thus the great study of life – and is about achieving the correct balance of foods.

The macrobiotic philosophy also encourages local foods to be eaten as available each season. This diet is excellent for keeping healthy dogs in good condition. However it should not be given to dogs with heart, kidney or thyroid problems as the seaweeds and tahini have a high sodium content.

PUTTING A MEAL TOGETHER

Soup, approximately 5 per cent
Grains, 50 per cent or more
Legumes and Seeds, more or less 10 per cent
Vegetables and Sea Vegetables, about 25 per cent
Animal-quality Food, 5 per cent or no more than 10 per cent
Seasoning
Desserts, Fruits and Nuts, a moderate 5 per cent
Drinks

from *The Practically Macrobiotic Cookbook*
by Keith Michell

This is a guide to balancing the type of food used in a macrobiotic meal. If you do want to include meat (animal-quality food), use it 'as a condiment'. George Ohsawa who is responsible for introducing the macrobiotic way of life to the Western world believes: 'If it can protest or run away – don't eat it!' Clearly he didn't have dogs in mind when he said that ...

MORNING MUSE

2 oz (55g/$\frac{1}{3}$ cup) brown rice, cooked in boiling water for 30–35
  minutes
1 teaspoon green nori flakes
3 dates, pitted and chopped
1 teaspoon sunflower seeds

Mix all the ingredients together.

MISSIS' MISO SOUP

'The Nannies gave Missis a big lunch to keep her strength up, and Pongo a big lunch in case he should feel neglected (as the fathers of expected puppies sometimes do), and then both dogs had a long afternoon nap on the best sofa.'

from *The Hundred and One Dalmatians*
by Dodie Smith

10 fl oz (285ml) water
1 teaspoon wakame, soaked in cold water for ten minutes
1 oz (30g) carrots, sliced
1 oz (30g) cabbage, shredded
1 oz (30g) leek, sliced
1 teaspoon mugi miso, mixed with 1 tablespoon hot water
2 oz (55g) tofu, cubed
1 oz (30g) soba buckwheat noodles, cooked in boiling water until swollen and tender

Put the carrots, cabbage and onion in a saucepan with the water. Bring to the boil and simmer for eight minutes. Add the mugi miso, tofu and buckwheat noodles. Gently heat up the soup – do not let it boil as this could damage the enzymes in the miso. Take off the burner and allow to cool slightly before serving.

RED SETTER RICE

'Hungry dogs will eat dirty pudding.'

Proverb

5 fl oz (140ml) water
5 fl oz (140ml) organic apple juice
1 tablespoon raisins
$\frac{1}{4}$ teaspoon cinnamon, ground
3 oz (85g) red cabbage, shredded
2 oz (55g/$\frac{1}{3}$ cup) brown rice, cooked in boiling water for 30–35 minutes
2 oz (55g) Vegan Crumble (page 128)

Put all the ingredients in a casserole dish. Bake for two hours at 250°F. Top with Vegan Crumble.

DASHING GOOD TEA

Queen Victoria owned many dogs in her lifetime, including Collies, Dachshunds, Greyhounds, Pomeranians, a Pekinese and a Tibetan Mastiff, but her first was a Spaniel called Dash.

'9 January 1839
I sent for Dashy, who Lord [Melbourne] accused of having crooked legs, which I wouldn't allow! We put him on the table and he was very much petted and admired by Lord M, who was so funny about him! We gave him tea and Lord M said, 'I wonder if lapping is a pleasant sensation,' - for that is a thing we had never felt.'
from *More Leaves from the Journal of a Life in the Highlands*
by Queen Victoria

2 strips of kombu
20 fl oz (570ml) water
1 teaspoon tamari soy sauce

Put the kombu and water in a saucepan. Bring to the boil and simmer for 25 minutes. Take out the kombu and add tamari soy sauce. Allow to cool before serving.

(Dashi is a macrobiotic broth made with kombu!)

When Dash died in 1840, Queen Victoria had the following epitaph engraved on his tombstone at Adelaide Lodge:

'His attachment was without selfishness
His playfulness without malice
His fidelity without deceit
Reader, if you would live beloved and die regretted, profit by the example of Dash.'

BARNEY'S BARLEY STEW

This is the dog,
That worried the cat,
That killed the rat,
That ate the malt
That lay in the house
that Jack built.

The House That Jack Built
Traditional Nursery Rhyme

Jeannie says: 'Barney Blundell was a mischievous yellow Labrador Retriever who belonged to my godparents and was always in trouble. He stole sausages from the local butcher, wellington boots from neighbours' porches and if the milkman left a carton of cream on anyone's doorstep within the vicinity, Barney always got to it first on one of his early morning raids. Nobody was immune from Barney's antics – he even stole a policeman's hat and ran down the beach and dropped it in the sea. But Toffee Mabey, a yappy French Bulldog/Yorkshire Terrier cross, came off worst. Toffee annoyed Barney so much so that one day he picked him up by the scruff of his neck, carried him into the sea and dunked him three or four times. We were to discover shortly afterwards that Toffee had swallowed what seemed like gallons of sea water … !'

1 oz (30g) carrot, grated
1 oz (30g) onion, chopped
2 oz (55g) cabbage, shredded
1 teaspoon unrefined sunflower oil
2 oz (55g) pearl barley, cooked in boiling water for 30 minutes

Fry the carrot, onion and cabbage in the sunflower oil for five minutes. Add the pearl barley.

A MORSEL FOR BULLSEYE

Bill Sikes, the villain in Charles Dickens' *Oliver Twist*, had a Bull Terrier called Bullseye.

'There was a fire in the tap-room, and some country-labourers were drinking before it. They made room for the stranger, but he sat down in the farthest corner, and ate and drank alone, or rather with his dog, to whom he cast a morsel of food from time to time.'

from *Oliver Twist*
by Charles Dickens

8 oz (230g) tofu, mashed
1 tablespoon parsley, chopped
1 oz (30g) onion, chopped
$\frac{1}{2}$ clove garlic, crushed
1 tablespoon tamari soy sauce
1 oz (30g) oatbran and wheatgerm
3 oz cabbage, shredded

Mix all the ingredients together except the cabbage. Place the mixture in a small loaf tin and bake in the oven for 1 hour at 350°F. Remove the contents from the tin, break the tofu mixture into small portions and mix with the cabbage.

NIPPER NOSH

If your dog appears to be suffering from boredom or depression, especially if you are out for the greater part of the day (when your dog would like to hear his owner's voice), music can ease the situation. Dogs particularly like classical music and opera. Alternatively you could put on an animal video as you leave the house – it will help your pet relax and not feel so lonely.

3 oz (85g) bulghur wheat, soaked in boiling water for 30 minutes
1 stick of celery, chopped
3 oz (85g) carrot, thinly sliced
2 oz (55g) mushrooms, chopped
4 oz (115g) tofu
6 fl oz (170ml) Dashing Good Tea (page 136)

Mix together the bulghur wheat, celery, carrot and mushrooms and place in a casserole dish. Put the tofu and Dashing Good Tea in a blender. When it's smooth, pour over the ingredients in the casserole dish. Bake in the oven at 350°F for 30 minutes.

COLOURFUL CABBAGE

'Folks either must avoid temptation
Or face my nasal accusation.'

from *The Bloodhound*
by Thomas Hood

2 oz (55g/$\frac{1}{3}$ cup) brown rice, cooked in boiling water for 30–35 minutes
4 oz (115g) red cabbage, shredded
1 apple, cored and chopped
1 tablespoon onion, chopped
$\frac{1}{4}$ teaspoon mint, chopped

Mix all the ingredients together.

> There are over forty varieties of mint – the most popular being spearmint (otherwise known as common garden mint). Mint helps digestion and its aroma enhances both man and dog's appetite. Mint has been grown for centuries and we learn from Pliny that the Romans particularly fancied this herb: 'The smell of Mint does stir up the minde ... It is applied with salt to the bitings of mad dogs.'
>
> Raw cabbage is particularly good for a dog suffering from anaemia.

WALLY WAKAME

'At one side of this lake, a string of gay rowboats shifted back and forth in the currents of the green water. Each boat had the name of a girl painted on its side, and from the end of the pier to which they were tied I went swimming while Wally, my dachshund, slept in one of the boats, in the shade of the bench that spans the center. Wally disliked sun and water.'

from *Small Beer* – 'Dog Story'
by Ludwig Bemelmans

2 oz (55g) bulghur wheat, soaked in boiling water for 30 minutes
1 oz bean sprouts, soaked in cold water for ten minutes
1 teaspoon wakame, soaked in cold water for ten minutes
1 teaspoon tahini
$\frac{1}{4}$ teaspoon tamari soy sauce

Mix all the ingredients together.

'Sea vegetables contain more minerals than any other kind of food.'

Professor Arasaki of Tokyo University

TAHINI

4 oz (115g) sesame seeds, ground
$\frac{1}{2}$ clove garlic, crushed
1 tablespoon unrefined sesame oil
juice of $\frac{1}{2}$ a lemon
2 fl oz (55ml) water

Put all the ingredients in a blender and mix until you have a smooth consistency, adjusting the water accordingly.

SCHNAUZER SPINACH

In David Marr's book, *Life of Patrick White* we learn that people who love Schnauzers say they 'are demanding, intelligent and so loyal that they haunt their owners' footsteps like pepper-and-salt ghosts'. P.V.M. White and E.G. Lascaris were responsible for reintroducing the Schnauzer to Australia in the late '40s, where their particular strain of breed became noted at the Royal Easter Show held annually in Sydney.

4 oz (115g) spinach, steamed
$\frac{1}{4}$ teaspoon extra virgin olive oil
2 oz (55g/$\frac{1}{3}$ cup) brown rice, cooked in boiling water for 30–35 minutes
1 tablespoon fresh wholemeal breadcrumbs
1 tablespoon natural wheatgerm
1 fl oz (30ml) Veggie Brew (page 101)

Mix the spinach, olive oil and brown rice together and put in a casserole dish. Mix together the breadcrumbs and wheatgerm and put on top of the spinach/rice mixture. Pour the Veggie Brew over the contents of the casserole dish and bake for 25 minutes at 350°F.

Your dog might appreciate a little Parmesan cheese sprinkled on top before baking.

SHIITAKE CHICKEN

'It was love at first sight. Without even bothering to eat the chicken, he came bounding to her and they were away into a wood together before anyone could stop them.'

from *The Hundred and One Dalmations*
by Dodie Smith

2 oz (55g) free range chicken breast, cut up into bite-sized pieces
3 shiitake mushrooms, soaked in water for 20 minutes and chopped
8 fl oz (230g) organic apple juice
$\frac{1}{4}$ teaspoon tamari soy sauce
1 oz (30g) brown rice, uncooked

Put all the ingredients in a casserole dish. Cover and bake in the oven for one hour at 400°F.

Shiitake mushrooms are high in protein and in Keith Michell's *The Practically Macrobiotic Cookbook* he recommends Shiitake Tea 'to help the discharge of yang from eating too much animal food, fish, buckwheat or salt, but should be taken only every few days'. This applies to man as well as dogs so a little Shiitake Tea occasionally would be good for you and your pet. This is how Keith Michell makes it:

SHIITAKE TEA

Boil two or three shiitake mushrooms in water for 15 or 20 minutes. Remove the mushrooms and drink the 'tea'.

It was interesting to read in Dr Andrew Weil's book *Natural Health, Natural Medicine* that 'shiitake [mushrooms] are free of the natural carcinogens found in the common white cultivated mushroom'.

LUATH'S NETTLE SOUP

Luath was the name of the yellow Labrador Retriever in Sheila Burnford's remarkable story, *The Incredible Journey*. It tells the harrowing tale of three faithful friends, two dogs and a cat, who travel alone through miles of Canadian wilderness to reach their home.

'The young dog too was hungry, but would have to be on the verge of starvation before the barriers of deep rooted Labrador heredity would be broken down. For generations his ancestors had been bred to retrieve without harming and there was nothing of the hunter in his makeup, and as yet, any killing was abhorrent to him. He drank deeply at the stream and urged his companions on.'

from *The Incredible Journey*
by Sheila Burnford

$\frac{1}{2}$ onion, finely chopped
$\frac{1}{2}$ teaspoon unrefined sesame oil
2 oz (55g) nettles, finely chopped
$\frac{1}{4}$ teaspoon tamari soy sauce
16 fl oz (455ml/1 USA pint) water
3 oz (85g) KemKibble

Sauté the onions in the sesame oil in a saucepan for four minutes. Add the nettles, soy sauce and water. Bring to the boil and simmer for 25 minutes. Top with KemKibble.

The word tamari can be traced as far back as A.D. 776 in Japan and it is used to describe the natural traditional way of fermenting soybeans as opposed to the chemically processed soy sauces. Keith Michell tells us that tamari 'is the liquid which rose to the surface of soybean hishio miso during fermentation.'

145

MILLIE'S MILLET

3 oz (85g/$\frac{1}{2}$ cup) millet grain
1 teaspoon unrefined safflower oil
11 fl oz (315ml/1$\frac{1}{2}$ cups) Dashing Good Tea (page 136)
2 oz (55g) cauliflower florets, chopped
2 oz (55g) red cabbage, shredded
1 oz (30g) red kidney beans, soaked in cold water for 12 hours, drained, boiled in fresh water for ten minutes, then simmered for 35 minutes

Fry the millet grain in safflower oil for five minutes, stirring all the time. Add Dashing Good Tea, cauliflower and cabbage. Cover and simmer for 15–20 minutes. Add the kidney beans.

VITAMINS, MINERALS AND NUTRITION

If you want your dog to be vegetarian, vegan or macrobiotic, a knowledge of foods and their vitamin and mineral content is essential to create a balanced diet. We have therefore compiled for you the following vitamin and mineral lists, explaining the foods in which to find them and how they are used by the body.

VITAMINS

	Source	Value
A	cheese, cod liver oil, milk & vegetables	bone growth, vision & skin
B1 Thiamine	beans, grain, peas, & offal	essential for appetite & digestion
B2 Riboflavin	milk, beef, chicken, liver & nuts	necessary for puppy growth, helps to absorb iron, protein, fat & carbohydrate energy levels
B3 Niacin	liver, fish, meat, & cereal grains	enzymes associated with metabolism, aids in building brain cells and in protein

B6
Pyridoxine	cereal grains, meat & vegetables	promotes circulation & digestion
B12	eggs, offal & wheatgerm	known as the anti-anaemic vitamin
C	fruit & vegetables	boosts the immune system (dogs produce their own Vitamin C, but extra aids their well-being)
D	cod liver oil, eggs & meat	helps bone growth in conjunction with calcium
E	cereals & green vegetables	maintaining cells, skin & nails
Beta-carotene	carrots	contains Vitamin A, good for urinary infections, eyes & lungs
Biotin	meat & vegetables	metabolism of amino acids
Choline	egg yolk, grains & liver	metabolism of fat
Folic Acid	green vegetables & wheat	essential for red blood cells & good for digestion absorption
Pantothenic Acid	nearly all foods	energy & cell growth

N.B. Specific attention must be paid not to overdose on Vitamins A or D. B Vitamins act as anti-depressants helping to keep your dog happy.

MINERALS

	Source	*Value*
Calcium	bones, bread, cheese & milk	bones, teeth, nerves, blood clotting
Copper	bones & meat	haemoglobin, skin & coat
Iodine	fish & vegetables	manufactures thyroid hormones
Iron	bread, eggs, cereals, meat & green vegetables	haemoglobin, metabolism of energy, respiration
Magnesium	bones, green vegetables & cereals	for development of bones, teeth and soft tissues, maintaining a healthy energy metabolism & digestive tract
Manganese	whole grains	metabolism of fat
Phosphorus	bones, fish, meat & whole grains	works in conjunction with calcium for bones & teeth

Potassium	meat & milk	nerves, water balance, painful joints & a dandruffy coat
Selenium	cereals, fish & meat, Brazil nuts	anti-cancer in conjunction with Vitamins A, C & E, good for skin & blood pressure
Sodium Chloride	cereals & salt	water balance
Zinc	whole grains, brewer's yeast, meat & pumpkin seeds	aids digestion, tissue repair & skin, helps maintain correct levels of Vitamin A in the blood

N.B.
Zinc supplements should be given separately from other vitamins/minerals.
Care should always be taken not to over-supplement when a dog's diet is sufficient in nutrients. That is why the Canine Care Vitamin/Mineral Supplement is the answer.

NUTRITIONAL FOOD VALUES

(Main Components)

Alfalfa	Vitamin C, B, D, E & K, calcium & phosphorus
All Bran	fibre, Vitamins A, B, C, D, iron & minerals
Apples	fibre, Vitamin C, E, B & potassium
Bananas	fibre, Vitamins C, E, B6 & potassium
Beef	protein, fat, Vitamin B12, niacin, thiamin, riboflavin & iron
Beans, Green	fibre, carbohydrate, Vitamins C, B, potassium & iron
Lima	fibre, protein, Vitamins E, B & minerals
Beetroot	fibre, Vitamins C, E, B, potassium & iron
Bones	minerals, calcium & phosphorus
Bran	thiamine & fibre
Bread	carbohydrate, fibre, sodium, Vitamin B & iron
Broccoli	fibre, protein, Vitamins C, A, E, B, calcium & magnesium
Brussels Sprouts	fibre, carbohydrate, protein, Vitamins C, E, B & iron
Bulghur	carbohydrate, protein, Vitamin B & minerals
Cabbage	fibre, Vitamins C, E, B & minerals
Carrots	carbohydrate, Vitamins A, C, E, B, & minerals

Cauliflower	fibre, Vitamins C, B & minerals
Celery	fibre, Vitamins C, B & potassium
Cheese	protein, fat, calcium, Vitamin B12 & zinc
Chicken	protein, fat, Vitamins E, B, B12 & minerals
Chicken Livers	Vitamins A, B, B12, C, E, protein, iron, fat & zinc
Cod	protein, fat, Vitamins E, B, B12, potassium & sodium
Cod Liver Oil	Vitamin D, A, phosphorus, iodine & sulphur
Corn	carbohydrate, fibre, protein, Vitamins C, E & B
Cornmeal	fibre, carbohydrate, Vitamins B, E, sodium, iron & fat
Corn Oil	fat, Vitamin E
Cottage Cheese	protein, fat, iron, Vitamins B12, B & calcium
Courgette/Zuchini	fibre, Vitamins A, C, B & potassium
Cucumber	Vitamins C, E, B & potassium
Dates	fibre, carbohydrate, Vitamin B, potassium & iron
Eggs	protein, fat, Vitamins D, E, B, B12 & iron
Flour, Wholemeal	carbohydrate, protein, fibre, Vitamin B & iron
Garlic	carbohydrate, potassium & calcium
Honey	carbohydrate, riboflavin, iron & potassium
Kelp	Vitamins A, B, C, D, E & K & iodine
Kidneys	protein, Vitamins B12, B, A, iron, zinc & fat
Lamb	protein, fat, Vitamins B12, B, E & minerals
Lentils	protein, Vitamins C, E, B, iron & potassium & phosphorus
Lettuce	fibre, Vitamins A, C, E, & potassium
Liver	protein, fat, Vitamins A, B12, B, C, D, E, iron & zinc
Macaroni	carbohydrate, protein, Vitamins E, B & iron
Meat	protein, fat, vitamins & minerals
Milk	carbohydrate, protein, fat, vitamins & minerals
Mushrooms	fibre, Vitamins C, E, B, potassium & iron
Nettles	Vitamin C & iron
Nuts	fat, protein, Vitamins E & Bs
Oats	carbohydrate, protein, Vitamin B, magnesium & iron
Oils	fat, essential fatty acids, Vitamin E

Onion	Vitamin C & minerals
Parsley	Vitamin A, C, iron, potassium & calcium phosphorus & manganese
Pasta	carbohydrate, protein, Vitamins E, B & iron
Peas	fibre, carbohydrate, protein, Vitamins C, B & potassium
Poppy Seeds	carbohydrate, fat, protein, calcium, phosphorus, potassium, sodium & magnesium
Potatoes	carbohydrate, phosphorus, potassium, iron, Vitamins C & B6
Pumpkin Seeds	fat, protein, carbohyrdate, calcium, phosphorus, iron & Vitamin A
Rabbit	protein, Vitamins B12, B, iron & minerals
Rice, Brown	carbohydrate, fibre, Vitamin E & minerals
Sesame Seeds	fat, carbohydrate, calcium, phosphorus, potassium & iron, Vitamins A, B1 & B2
Spinach	fibre, carbohydrate, protein, Vitamins A, C, E, B & iron
Sunflower Seeds	fat, Vitamins E & B
Tahini	fat, carbohydrate, calcium, phosphorus, iron, potassium, Vitamins A, B1 & B2
Tofu	protein, fat, Vitamins B1 & B2, magnesium, calcium, phosphorus & iron & potassium
Tomato Purée	carbohydrate, Vitamins A, C, B, sodium, potassium & iron
Tripe	protein & fat
Tuna	protein, fat, iron & sodium
Turkey	protein, fat, Vitamins B12, B, E, zinc, iron & potassium
Turnips	fibre, carbohydrate, Vitamins A, C, E, B & potassium
Wakame	carbohydrate, calcium, phosphorus, iron, sodium, potassium, iodine, Vitamins A & C
Yeast	protein, Vitamin B – thiamine & riboflavin, calcium & iron
Yogurt	protein, fat, Vitamin B12, riboflavin & calcium

OKAY OILS

The best oils for cooking are unrefined, cold-pressed oils. Although they may be more expensive than other oils, you will find you don't have to use as much. The cold-pressed form of olive oil is called 'extra-virgin' – if it refers to 'pure' that means petro-chemical extraction. Avoid solvent-expressed oils – by the time the chemical solvent, caustic soda and bleaching processes have done their worst, there is not much goodness left. If you can get hold of them, coconut oil and palm oil are excellent for cooking at high temperatures, followed by extra virgin olive oil for moderate heat, and sesame seed oil and flax-seed oil for low-heat cooking. Corn oil, grapeseed oil, groundnut oil, safflower oil and sunflower oil can also be used in any of the recipes in this book. When using oil for stir-frying, add a little water to the oil, as this stops the oil molecules from overheating. Otherwise check the proportion of saturates, mono-unsaturates and poly-unsaturates: oils with a high saturate and mono-unsaturate content are better for heating than those with a high poly-unsaturate content. Always store oils in a cool, dark place.

DRINK OR TREAT

'He who drinks a little too much drinks much too much.'
Proverb

'Toto was not grey; he was a little black dog, with long silky hair and small black eyes that twinkled merrily on either side of his funny, wee nose.

... and taking a pail from the shelf, she carried it down to the little brook and filled it with clear, sparkling water ... having helped herself and Toto to a drink of the cool, clear water, she set about making ready for the journey to the City of Emeralds.'

from *The Wizard of Oz*
by L. Frank Baum

Have you ever questioned what is actually coming out of your taps? The mineral content in water varies from region to region and some areas treat their water supply with chemicals. When Bob Mann, a parrot breeder near Peterborough, found his baby parrots were all dying he did a thorough investigation and traced the problem to his local reservoir. In the hot summer the nitrites, nitrates and chlorides had risen far above the acceptable levels and had poisoned the baby parrots. Because of the amount of chlorine and fluoride in most tap water, we advocate bottled or filtered water. Make sure the bottled water you purchase has been purified by a natural method. Also some plastic bottles can have an adverse effect on health, so whenever possible buy water in glass bottles. This too has the added advantage that they can be recycled.

	Chloride	Nitrate	Sodium
Ballygowan	28.0	9.0	15.0
Buxton	42.0	0.1	24.0
Caledonian	8.0	2.0	6.8
Chiltern Hills	15.0	5.0	8.0
Evian	4.5	3.8	5.0
Highland Spring	7.5	1.0	6.0
Strathmore	125.0	5.0	46.0
Vittel	–	0.6	7.3
Volvic	8.4	6.3	9.4
Welsh Mineral Water	12.0	1.3	5.0

If you can afford bottled water, do check the contents and make sure it has the lowest possible amount of chlorides, nitrates and sodium. An excessive amount of sodium in a dog's diet is bad for animals with a heart condition or diabetes and can also lead to hypertension. If you haven't already studied a typical analysis of bottled water, you will be amazed at the differences between the brands.

Throughout the day a dog loses water through panting, urine and faeces, depending on how much exercise it has and the climate. It is essential that this water be replaced. However, it is also important to keep an eye on how much water your dog drinks, because an excessive amount can indicate the early signs of a disease.

The following is a guideline:

Dog's Weight	Daily Water Requirement
	(from various sources, i.e. moisture contained in food)
30 – 50 pounds	1 – 1 1/2 pints
70 – 90 pounds	2 – 3 pints

Some people may have been guilty of offering their dogs a taste of alcohol for fun, but it can be harmful and is not advised. An exception for dogs in distress would be neat Bach Rescue Remedy which contains brandy.

> 'Last week was one of sadness. Charley dog died full of years but leaving a jagged hole nevertheless. He died of what would probably be called cirrhosis in a human. This degeneration is usually ascribed to indulgence in alcohol. But Charley did not drink, or if he did he was very secret about it.'
>
> from *Last Days*, a letter to D.E.S. Montgomery, April 1963
> by John Steinbeck

It is best not to get in the habit of feeding your dog between meals and to resist the pleading eyes at the dinner table. If you have left-overs from your meal, provided they are not highly seasoned, spicy or sugary, keep them for your dog's next meal.

> 'Jesus replied, 'It is not right to take the children's bread and throw it to the dogs.' 'True, sir,' she answered; 'and yet the dogs eat the scraps that fall from their masters' table.'
>
> from *The New English Bible: New Testament*
> Matthew 15, verses 26 and 27

Treats should be used only as a reward for good behaviour and then given sparingly – as food and over-indulgence can lead to obesity and all the ensuing problems. Raw carrots, apples, grapes, cucumber and even dried fruits make a healthy alternative, and have you tried air-popped popcorn?

Although most dogs will jump at the chance of eating chocolate, it contains the stimulant theobromine which, if given to dogs in large quantities, can act as a poison. Baking chocolate has nearly nine times the amount of theobromine as milk chocolate. This is not to say don't ever give your dog chocolate, but try substituting with carob-based treats. Carob looks like and tastes like chocolate but has no refined sugar or caffeine.

> 'She gave him rich dainties
> Whenever he fed,
> And erected a monument
> When he was dead.'
>
> from *Old Mother Hubbard and Her Dog*
> Traditional Nursery Rhyme

L'EAU GLACÉ

Chacun à son goût!

1 bowl of natural spring water (preferably bottled in France!)
2 ice cubes
squeeze of lemon juice

Combine all the ingredients in a drinking bowl. Allow the ice to melt. Serve.

> On a more serious note, if your dog is suffering from severe dehydration try offering him an ice cube to suck before he consumes vast quantities of liquid which could make him sick.

> Giving a puppy an ice cube to chew on will help ease the pain of teething.

ALBUMEN WATER

1 free range egg
1 teaspoon glucose powder
water

Boil some water and let it cool. Beat the egg white together with the glucose powder and a tablespoon of water.

> If your dog suffers from travel sickness this concoction could help ease the problem.

HONEY WATER

20 fl oz (570ml/2 ½ cups) water
1 tablespoon honey

Boil the water, stir in the honey. Let it cool. Serve.

If you are feeding your dog a dry-mixer all-in-one food the addition of honey water will make it far more palatable and nutritious. Honey is easily digested and goes straight into the bloodstream because it has already been pre-digested by bees and is therefore a quick source of energy. If your dog is known to suffer from hypoglycemia (low blood sugar), an emergency measure could be to rub honey on its gums. Honey is also a good tonic for heart and nervous conditions.

BARLEY WATER

20 fl oz (570ml/2 ½ cups) water
1 tablespoon pearl barley

Boil the water, add the pearl barley and simmer for 25 minutes. Allow to cool before straining off the liquid. Serve.

This drink is rich in magnesium and helps to purify the blood so it is an excellent remedy if your dog is suffering from a skin complaint or rheumatism. If your dog has a kidney disease or is showing signs of not digesting its food properly (such as severe diarrhoea and a decrease in weight) barley water should be its only intake of liquid. To make it a bit more appetising one can add honey (1 tablespoon per pint of liquid).

OLD YELLER OAT MILK

Jeannie says: 'Part of growing up in the States was being introduced at an early age to *Old Yeller* by Fred Gipson, the first moving book about a dog that really captured one's imagination and brought emotions to the surface. I can still see Mrs Heinisch, our teacher, in tears at the end of the book every time she read it to her class of eight-year-olds.'

4 oz (115g) oats
40 fl oz water
a pinch of salt
1 tablespoon honey or maple syrup
1 teaspoon unrefined grapeseed oil

Heat the water to near-boiling and pour over the oats. Let this mixture stand overnight. Strain off the liquid. Add a pinch of salt, the honey and grapeseed oil to the 'oat milk'. Reheat till luke-warm.

Oats should be an important ingredient in every dog's diet, particularly stud dogs and brood bitches. This grain provides a good source of iron and at the same time acts as an excellent agent for cleansing the intestines. Oats can be used as a tonic for dogs suffering from a nervous condition. This drink would be beneficial to any dog feeling a little under-the-weather.

SCAP'S TEA

Sir Edward Elgar had a dog called Scap and he wrote to his friend Dr Charles Buck on 8 January 1886 telling him of Scap's condition:

'Scap has had a cough during the last fortnight – I have taken him to a Vet: (a good one) and he (Scap) has had a few pills; he is all right again now. He had the mug & the beefbone on Xmas day; ... '

from *Edward Elgar: Letters of a Lifetime*
ed. Jerrold Northrop Moore
(Oxford University Press 1990)

4 oz (115g) lean minced beef
10 fl oz (285ml/1 $\frac{1}{4}$ cups) water
1 teaspoon Marmite (Vegemite, Vitamite or Yeast Extract)

Put the beef, water and Marmite in a saucepan. Bring to the boil and simmer for 45 minutes. Strain through a colander, saving the liquid. Scap's Tea should be served warm.

SCAP'S SCRAPS

The boiled meat from Scap's Tea can be saved and served with a small amount of cooked vegetables and KemKibble (page 188), Crunchy Crumbs or Chunchy Chunks (page 176) to make a meal in itself.

TIPPY DAWS DOG BISCUITS

1 1b (455g/4 cups) Singleton stoneground wholemeal flour*
9 oz (255g/1 $\frac{3}{4}$ cups) bulghur wheat
3 oz (85g/1 cup) oats with bran
3 oz (85g/1 $\frac{1}{4}$ cups) dried skimmed milk
2 tablespoons dried parsley
$\frac{1}{2}$ teaspoon garlic granules
1 $\frac{1}{2}$ teaspoons dried yeast
12 fl oz (340ml/1 $\frac{1}{2}$ cups) Meaty Brew, Fish Brew or Veggie Brew
(pages 62, 93, 101)
1 free range egg, beaten

Mix all the dry ingredients together, add the brew and egg. Knead and roll out to $\frac{1}{4}$" or $\frac{1}{2}$" depending on the size of dog. Using a dog-shaped cutter make the biscuits and place on a floured baking tray. Bake at 300°F for 35–40 minutes. Cool on a rack, or if you want the biscuits extra-hard, turn the oven off and let them dry out on the baking tray in the oven for five to seven hours.

* The Singleton stoneground wholemeal flour is produced in the Lurgashall Mill which is now sited at the Weald & Downland Museum in Singleton, West Sussex.

CRAB STRAWS

In Shakespeare's *The Two Gentlemen of Verona*, Proteus' clownish servant, Lance, has a dog called Crab, who seems to become the star of the show in any production . It was no exception at the opening performance at the 'new' Globe Theatre in London on 20 August 1996: Crab made his entrance, had a barking fit, ate some straw, relieved himself on one of the Corinthian columns and then attempted to join the audience! Nothing had changed since 1644 ...

4 oz (115g/1 cup) superfine self-raising wholemeal flour
$2\frac{1}{2}$ oz (70g) soy margarine
1 oz (30g) Cheddar cheese, grated
1 oz (30g) crab in brine, drained
1 teaspoon bonemeal
1 egg yolk
2–3 tablespoons cold spring water

Rub the soy margarine into the flour until the mixture resembles breadcrumbs. Add the Cheddar cheese, crab and bonemeal. Combine the egg yolk and water before adding to the other ingredients. Mix until you have a stiff dough. Knead on a floured surface and roll out as thinly as possible. Cut into $\frac{1}{4}$" wide and 2" long strips. Place on a greased baking tray and bake at 400°F for 12 minutes. Allow to cool on a rack.

KEEP-OUT-OF-TROUBLE TREATS

'There was a fat, funny boy-puppy called Roly-Poly, who was always getting into mischief.'

from *The Hundred and One Dalmatians*
by Dodie Smith

2 $\frac{1}{4}$ oz (65g/1 cup) All Bran

4 oz (115g/1 cup) dried mixed fruit – raisins, sultanas, currants, chopped apricots, chopped pineapple etc.

8 fl oz (230ml/1 cup) goats' milk

4 oz (115g/1 cup) stoneground self-raising wholemeal flour

Mix the All Bran and dried fruit together. Add the milk. Leave to soak for an hour. Add the flour. Mix thoroughly. Spread the mixture evenly in a greased tin or dish approximately 8" × 6" (20cm × 15cm). Bake for 45 minutes at 325°F. Take it out of container and cool on a rack. Cut into strips about 3" × 1" (7.5cm × 2.5cm) or halve that if you have a small dog. Serve as a special treat or to dogs who need high-fibre in their diet.

SCOTTY SNACKS

In James Thurber's *Fables For Our Time* we learn from 'The Scotty Who Knew Too Much' that 'it's better to ask some questions than to know all the answers'.

4 oz (115g) sultanas
4 fl oz (115ml) hot water
8 oz (230g/2 cups) superfine self-raising wholemeal flour
1/2 teaspoon cinnamon
1/2 teaspoon nutmeg
1 teaspoon honey
a pinch of garlic granules
8 oz (230g) oats with bran
2 free range eggs
4 fl oz (115ml) unrefined grapeseed oil
1 teaspoon vanilla

Soak the sultanas in the hot water. Mix the flour, spices and garlic granules. Blend in the oats and honey. Beat the eggs with a fork. Add the grapeseed oil, undrained sultanas and vanilla. Pour the mixture into the dry ingredients. Stir until blended. Drop tea-spoonfuls on an ungreased baking tray. Bake at 360°F for 12–15 minutes. Cool on a rack.

FUSSIE FISH FINGERS

10 oz (285g/2 ½ cups) stoneground wholemeal flour
10 oz (285g/2 ½ cups) cornmeal
1 tablespoon dried parsley
1 teaspoon Parmesan cheese, grated
8-ounce (230g) can 'dolpin friendly' tuna steak in vegetable oil
4 fl oz (115ml/½ cup) Fish Brew (page 93)
4 fl oz (115ml/½ cup) unrefined grapeseed oil

Mix all the dry ingredients together. Drain and flake the tuna steak. Add the tuna, fish brew and grapeseed oil to the dry ingredients. Mix well. Roll out on a floured surface to ½". Using a fish-shaped cutter, form biscuits and place on a floured baking tray. Bake at 350°F for 30 minutes. Leave to cool on a rack.

> The actress Ellen Terry wrote fondly of one of her terriers, Fussie (who later became Sir Henry Irving's pet), in her book *The Story of My Life*. Fussie didn't acquire his name for nothing – he had a passion for 'ladies' fingers' soaked in champagne. So if you are feeling extravagant try dipping Fussie's Fish Fingers in champagne for a treat and substitute the salmon with tuna!

> Sadly food proved to be Fussie's final downfall. In 1897, during a rehearsal in Manchester, one of the carpenters threw down his coat, containing a ham sandwich in one of the pockets, and it fell down the open trap door. Fussie, getting a whiff of the ham sandwich, went in pursuit of it and fell through the trap door. She was killed instantly.

ARGUS' HEART-BREAK BISCUITS

In Greek mythology we learn from Homer about Ulysses' faithful dog, Argus. He waited twenty years to welcome his master back from the Trojan war. Ulysses returned in disguise and, not wishing to reveal his true identity, had to ignore Argus' wagging tail and pleading eyes. Broken-hearted by the rejection, Argus promptly died at his feet.

8 oz (230g) self-raising wholemeal flour
3 oz (85g) carob powder
1 oz (30g) brown rice flour
2 oz (55g) date and walnuts, dried and chopped
4 fl oz (115ml) unrefined sunflower oil
1 free range egg, beaten
4 tablespoons water

Mix the dry ingredients together and mix the liquids together. Combine the two until you have a dough you can roll out on a brown-rice floured surface. Cut $\frac{1}{4}$" thick dough into heart-shaped biscuits. Place on a baking tray and bake at 360°F for 25 minutes. Turn the oven off and allow the Argus' Heart-Break Biscuits to dry out on the baking tray for five to seven hours.

Juliette de Bairacli Levy in her book *The Complete Herbal Handbook for the Dog and Cat* suggests adding some carob powder to 'puppy and junior meal formula as a protection against hip dysplasia'. Carob is full of vitamins, minerals and natural sugars and you will find your dog loves the taste.

TREACLE WITH A SECRET

Treacle was the name of a Manchester Terrier belonging to Agatha Christie, the well-known writer of detective novels.

4 oz (115g) soy margarine
1 teaspoon honey
1 tablespoon Lyle's Golden Syrup
6 oz (140g) porridge oats with bran
4 oz (115g) organic wholemeal flour
1 teaspoon poppy seeds
1 pine kernel (your dog will get a surprise when he finds it!)
$\frac{1}{2}$ teaspoon natural wheatgerm
1 free range egg, beaten
2 fl oz (55ml) Veggie Brew (page 101)

Put the soy margarine, honey and Golden Syrup in a saucepan. Let the contents melt slowly over a low heat. Combine this liquid with all the other ingredients. Put the mixture in a small baking dish and cook in the oven for 25 minutes at 350°F.

SNOOPY NUT SNACKS

('Snoopy' is the seventh most popular dog name in the USA!)

'Charlotte: (To Pischik, who's stroking the dog's ears.) It eats nuts.
    Pischik (Withdrawing slightly.) Imagine.'

from *The Cherry Orchard*
by Anton Chekhov

12 oz (340g/3 cups) stoneground wholemeal flour
5 oz (140g/1 $\frac{1}{2}$ cups) Scottish whole rolled porridge oats
1 oz (30g/$\frac{1}{4}$ cup) dried goats' milk
1 oz (30g/$\frac{1}{4}$ cup) natural wheatgerm
$\frac{1}{2}$ teaspoon garlic granules
10 fl oz (285g/1 $\frac{1}{4}$ cups) Veggie Brew (page 101)
1 oz (30g) mixed nuts (walnuts, almonds, hazelnuts), chopped
1 free range egg, beaten

Mix all the dry ingredients together. Add the Veggie Brew and egg to the dry ingredients. Roll out on a floured surface to $\frac{1}{4}$" or $\frac{1}{2}$" thickness, depending on the size of your dog. Make snacks using a bone-shaped cutter. Place on a greased baking tray and bake in a 300°F oven for one hour.

> Most dogs find nuts tasty and have even been known to crack the shells of walnuts and hazelnuts to extract the kernel. Nuts are rich in natural oils, vitamins and minerals. They are best served raw, either finely crushed into a powder or made into nut butter. Nut powder mixed with a little milk makes a nutritious tonic for thin dogs.

NOBLE BIRTHDAY CAKE

'My favourite collie Noble is always downstairs when we take our meals, and was so good, Brown making him lie on a chair or couch, and he never attempted to come down without permission, and even held a piece of cake in his mouth without eating it, till told he might.'

from *More Leaves from the Journal of a Life in the Highlands* by Queen Victoria

1 teaspoon extra virgin olive oil
3 oz (85g) chicken mince
$\frac{1}{2}$ oz (15g) onion, chopped
$\frac{1}{2}$ teaspoon garlic granules
$\frac{1}{2}$ teaspoon green nori flakes
2 oz (55g) superfine self-raising wholemeal flour
2 oz (55g) soy margarine
1 teaspoon honey
1 free range egg, beaten

Fry the chicken mince, onion and garlic granules in the olive oil for six to eight minutes, stirring occasionally. Combine with the nori flakes, wholemeal flour, soy margarine, honey and egg. Place the mixture in a baking tin approximately 6" × 3" (15cm × 7.5cm) and cook in the oven at 360°F for 25 minutes.

NOBLE LIVER ICING

$\frac{1}{2}$ teaspoon unrefined sesame oil
1 teaspoon onion, chopped
3 oz (85g) chicken livers, chopped
a pinch of rosemary, chopped
1 tablespoon natural Greek-style yogurt

Fry the onion, chicken livers and rosemary in the sesame oil for six to eight minutes, stirring occasionally. Put all the ingredients into a blender and combine until you have a smooth paste. Spread the Noble Liver Icing on the top of the Noble Birthday Cake. Invite some of your dog's best pals round to share this delicious concoction.

JO-FI CHRISTMAS CAKE

Sigmund Freud had a Chow Chow called Jo-Fi.

1 teaspoon unrefined safflower oil
1 ½ oz (45g) turkey mince
1 ½ oz (45g) chicken livers, chopped
¼ teaspoon sage, chopped
2 oz (55g) superfine self-raising wholemeal flour
2 oz (55g) soy margarine
1 teaspoon honey
1 free range egg, beaten
1 teaspoon cornmeal
1 oz (30g) dates and walnuts, dried and chopped
1 teaspoon Parmesan cheese, grated
1 banana, puréed and 1 glazed cherry

Fry the turkey mince, chicken livers and sage in the safflower oil for six to eight minutes, stirring occasionally. Combine the wholemeal flour and soy margarine. Blend in the honey, egg, cornmeal, dates and walnuts. Put the mixture in a baking tin approximately 6" × 3" (15cm × 7.5cm). Sprinkle the Parmesan cheese on top and bake at 375°F for 25 minutes.

Allow the cake to cool before spreading the banana purée on the top. Place the cherry in the centre.

> 'Kipper squeezed the flat thing into a cake shape and watched it bake in the oven. To his surprise it changed itself slowly into a sort of heap, but it smelled good. He put the last remaining cherry on the top for decoration.'
>
> from *Kipper's Birthday*
> by Mick Inkpen

LIVER TRAINING TREATS

16 oz (455g) liver
3 cloves garlic, crushed

Cut the liver into medium-sized pieces (they shrink during cooking). Mix with crushed garlic cloves. Place in a greased baking dish. Cover and bake in the oven at 325°F for two hours. Allow them to cool and harden.

> These make a welcome and healthy reward for dogs in training – they love them and will do virtually anything for you in order to get one!

SUGAR-FREE
SHAG SHAPES

Virginia Woolf had a Skye Terrier called Shag, who knew better than to accept any sugar in his diet:

'The solitary occasion when he [Shag] found it necessary to inflict marks of his displeasure on human flesh was once when a visitor rashly tried to treat him as an ordinary pet-dog and tempted him with sugar and called him "out of his name" by the contemptible lap-dog title of 'Fido'.'

from *On a Faithful Friend* (1904)
by Virginia Woolf

16 oz (455g) Shipton's organic light rye flour
12 oz (340g) Shipton's 5 Cereals Blend – malted wheat flakes, barley flakes, sunflower seeds, millet and oats or similar mix
3 oz (85g) dried milk powder
3 oz (85g) chicken livers, chopped
3 oz (85g) chicken, minced
2 teaspoons green nori flakes
1 teaspoon cold-pressed virgin sunflower oil
8 oz (230ml) Meaty Brew – made with chicken bones (page 62)
1 free range egg, beaten
1 tablespoon unrefined sesame oil
1 tablespoon fresh parsley, chopped

Mix together the rye flour, 5 Cereals Blend and milk powder. Fry the chicken livers, chicken and nori flakes in the sunflower oil for 10–12 minutes. Put the fried chicken livers, chicken and nori flakes in a blender with the Meaty Brew, egg, sesame oil and parsley. Combine until you have a smooth consistency. Add this to the dry ingredients and mix well until you have a stiff dough. Roll out on a floured board to approximately $\frac{1}{4}''$ thick. Using a dog-bone shape cutter, make as many shapes as you can. Place them on a baking try and cook in the oven at 350°F for 30 minutes. Cool on a rack or if you want extra-hard Shag Shapes, turn the oven off and allow them to dry out for five to seven hours in the oven.

Sugar-Free Shag Shapes *must* be stored in a refrigerator.

CHIHUAHUA CARROT CAKES

'For dinner they consume jellymeat, skeleton biscuits, a fairy cake, a portion of best carpet and a sock that is four days old.'

from *Dr Xargle's Book of Earth Hounds*
by Jeanne Willis & Tony Ross

1 free range egg, beaten
1 tablespoon honey
3 tablespoons unrefined sunflower oil
2 oz (55g) self-raising wholemeal flour
$\frac{1}{4}$ teaspoon cinnamon
$\frac{1}{4}$ teaspoon nutmeg
1 teaspoon desiccated coconut
1 teaspoon bonemeal
3 oz (85g) carrot, grated

Mix the honey and egg. Gradually add the sunflower oil, followed by all the other ingredients. Put the mixture into a 12-sectioned mini fairy cake baking tin and cook in the oven for 20–25 minutes at 360°F. Cool the cakes on a rack.

One advantage of coconut is that the chances of its having been chemical sprayed are virtually nil because of its hard outer shell. A little desiccated coconut added to your dog's meal once or twice a week will aid digestion, and the albumen contained in coconut is good for the blood corpuscles.

CAULIFLOWER ICING

Cook until tender 2 oz (55g) cauliflower florets in water flavoured with a $\frac{1}{4}$ teaspoon mugi miso. Drain and purée the cauliflower in a blender. Spread the Cauliflower Icing on top of the Chihuahua Carrot Cakes.

CRUNCHY CRUMBS

Take any amount of stale brown bread. Rub into breadcrumbs, not necessarily super-fine. Sprinkle the breadcrumbs on a large baking tray and bake in the oven for 30 minutes at 300°F. Crunchy Crumbs make a delicious topping for any meal and to vary them you can add ground nuts (Brazil nuts, hazelnuts etc.) or seeds (pumpkin, poppy, sunflower, etc.)

CRUNCHY CHUNKS

Slice any amount of wholemeal bread and cut into medium-sized chunks. Put on a baking tray and bake in the oven at 300°F for 45 minutes till crisp. You can add a bit of grated cheese to Crunchy Chunks to give your dog a different topping for his usual meal.

TASTERS' TITBITS

14 oz (400g) Singleton stoneground wholemeal flour
2 oz (55g) brown rice flour
4 oz (115g) bulghur wheat
3 oz (85g) oats with bran
1 oz (30g) rye flakes
1 oz (30g) toasted oatbran
1 oz (30g) barley flakes
1 oz (30g) corn meal
1 oz (30g) natural wheatgerm
1 tablespoon bonemeal
1 $\frac{1}{2}$ teaspoons dried yeast
2 oz (55g) dried skimmed milk
1 teaspoon garlic granules
1 tablespoon dried parsley
1 teaspoon poppy seeds
1 tablespoon pumpkin seeds
2 teaspoons sunflower seeds
1 oz (30g) organic carrot, grated
$\frac{1}{4}$ apple, finely chopped
1 tablespoon green nori flakes
12 fl oz (340ml) Meaty Brew, Fish Brew or Veggie Brew (pages 62, 93, 101) with 1 teaspoon Marmite
1 free range egg, beaten

Mix the dry ingredients together. Add all the other ingredients and mix thoroughly. Knead and roll out to $\frac{1}{4}$" or $\frac{1}{2}$" depending on the size of dog. Using bone-shaped cutter, make the biscuits and place on a floured baking tray. Bake at 300°F for 35–40 minutes. Turn the oven off and let the biscuits dry out in the oven for five-seven hours.

For a treat, mix a tablespoon of carob powder with $1\frac{1}{2}$ teaspoons water and spread on the biscuits. Put in the refrigerator to harden.

Makes about 36 biscuits – they should be stored in the refrigerator.

This recipe has been concocted as a thank you to all the dogs who have been willing tasters of the recipes in this book. We have tried to combine their favourite ingredients and, judging by how they all devoured these Titbits, we guess we got it right. It would be impossible to list all the dogs who have tried our dog food but we would like to give a special mention to the following:

Wilfred Ashby – Welsh Springer Spaniel
Bear and Mistie Ashcroft – Newfoundlands
Maisie Banfield – Wire-haired Dachshund
Zoe Barc – German Shepherd Dog/Labrador Retriever
Roscoe Bastedo – Dobermann
Charley Baxter – Labrador Retriever
Bertie Bentley – Golden Retriever
Luke Berridge – Labrador Retriever
Barty Blythe – Labrador/Collie Cross
Bigsby Boutwood – Labrador Retriever Cross
Ben Buchner – Alsatian
Liffey Butterworth – yellow Labrador Retriever
Troy Butterworth – Collie Cross
Bannock and Oliver Cammack – English Springer Spaniels
Bella Capelin – Border Terrier
Hamish Carswell – Golden Retriever/Collie
Penny Connell – Lurcher
Ollie Daniel – Lurcher
Sam Daniel – Collie
Tippy Daws – Collie/Mix
Bagheera Dembinsky – Labrador Retriever
Brett Denison – Welsh Corgi
Golly Deveries – Welsh Collie
Dudley Edward – English Springer Spaniel/Mix
Scrappy Elliott – Shih-Tzu/Jack Russell/Mix
Bertie Evans – Bernese Mountain Dog
Oscar Evans – Yorkshire Terrier
Scamp Farmer – Wire-haired Fox Terrier

Gary Flind – Pug
Sidney Flind – English Bull Terrier
Daisy and Araminta Gale – King Charles Spaniels
Daisy and Little Dorrit Garland – Dobermanns
Champers Goodwin – Lurcher
Kulu Green – Dobermann Pinscher Cross
Wooster Gudgeon – Labrador Retriever
Domino Hammond – Border Collie
Noodles Hardy – English Bull Terrier
Tessa Hedgecock – English Springer Spaniel
Darcy Heyes – English Setter
Holly Horne – English Springer Spaniel
Holly Houseman – Great Dane
Jade Howling – Rottweiler
Meg Leaver – Cavalier King Charles Spaniel
Jodie Lillywhite – yellow Labrador Retriever
Gemma Luffingham – Boxer
Andy Martin –Labrador Retriever
Sky Martin – English Bulldog
Bobby Mash – Cocker Spaniel
Dazy Mash – Cocker Spaniel
Buster Melling – English Springer Spaniel
Nell Meyer – Golden Retriever
Tor Moores – Labrador Retriever
Jade Morgan – Labrador Retriever
Poppy Oldham – Labrador Retriever
Milly Pine – Bearded Collie Cross
Fey and Tosh Prescott – Lurchers
Flynn Prescott – Greyhound
Waldo Remington – Collie Jack Russell Cross
Kilda Rhodes – Cairn Terrier
Percy Rowland – Yorkshire Terrier
Gromit Stickland – Jack Russell Terrier
Poppy and Rebecca Stoddard – Jack Russell Terriers
Satchmo Sweet – Labrador Retriever/English Springer Spaniel Cross
Daisy Timothy – Flat-coated Retriever
Millie Timothy – Golden Retriever
Morgan Timothy – Labrador Retriever
Sally Townsend – Greek Heinz 57

Della Turner – Minature Long-haired Dachshund
Zea Turner – Dobermann
Pippin Woolnough – Lurcher
Holly Wright – English Springer Spaniel
Fred and Snoopy Young – Basset Hounds

DIETS FOR DIFFERENT AGES

'You cannot teach old dogs new tricks.'

Proverb

Puppies, adolescents, adults and senior citizens – in the wild they would all have eaten the same things. However, they would have devoured a whole raw rabbit, pheasant, hare or partridge and these are the perfect foods. Animals fed on such a natural diet would experience very few health problems in old age. That isn't the case in our modern world of pollutants and pesticides, and puppies and older dogs therefore need different diets.

Puppies must eat the right things for optimum development and do not fare well on a cheap all-in-one dried food, semi-moist preparation or canned food. Equally, a senior citizen cannot cope with some of the impure foods an adolescent or adult can tolerate. If a dog is fed meals of minimum nutritional value its health is bound to suffer in later years. It will get heart problems, diabetes, thyroid, pancreatic and intestinal disorders, liver and kidney trouble or even cancer, unless the symptoms are spotted early and the diet changed.

Puppies aged between two and three months should be fed four meals a day. The proportions should be roughly 75 per cent to 25 per cent in the order in which the ingredients appear.

PERFECT PUPPY MENU

Morning
Weetabix and Goats' Milk

Mid-day
Scrambled Eggs and Raw Tripe

Afternoon
Cooked Chicken Mince and Biscuit Meal

Evening
Raw Tripe and Biscuit Meal

If you don't have time to make home-made meals adding good supplements of calcium and phosphorus and bonemeal, Pedigree Chum Puppy Food is recommended by the Akita breeder, Jo Gibbs. We suggest that for biscuit meal you use Beta Puppy Meal. Farley's Rusks and small raw carrots which can be given as treats and are particularly good for puppies' teeth.

Puppies aged between three and six months should have three meals a day; i.e. cut out the midday meal. At the age of nine months they have more or less stopped growing and should have one main meal or two smaller meals per day. A dog's digestive system takes about eight hours so you would be advised to feed the main meal in the morning. That way you won't have to get up in the middle of the night!

IDEAL ADULT DOG DIET

According to our research the majority of breeders, kennel owners and vets, advocate raw green tripe and plain biscuit as the main meal (50/50 ratio). Tripe is the part of the animal which is rich in grains and grasses, and in the wild a dog would always eat the stomach and liver of its prey first. There is a supreme irony in writing a book about healthy cooking for dogs and advocating the above recipe, but it would be unethical for us to do otherwise. Raw green tripe and plain biscuit are the healthiest meal. And the best treats are also natural – uncooked shank bones, raw carrots, cabbage, cauliflower and broccoli stalks are far better than crunchy chews that (if you read the small print) contain animal derivatives and sugars. The only exception we would make to this diet would be for an aggressive dog, who would fare better on a cooked chicken and rice or a totally vegetarian diet.

GERIATRIC DOG DIET

If a dog has been fed on raw green tripe all its life it should be unnecessary to change its food and longevity should be assured. However, if you have been taking short-cuts with inexpensive cans, dried foods or semi-moist meals then there is a possibility that there will be problems in later life. Vet Mark Elliott has come up with specific menus for particular diseases. If we had to pick one general recipe for an older dog it would be cooked chicken or rabbit with boiled brown rice and carrots and broccoli. If a dog is fed on 'instant' foods all its life its intestinal tract will be less than robust and a geriatric diet is called for.

If you have to feed an instant meal we recommend Pedigree Puppy cans and Denes in puppyhood, and for adults Naturediet or Butcher's Tripe and Chicken (contains 16 per cent tripe and 16 per cent chicken). Denes tins for the older dog are good, and of the dried foods the more expensive range like Hill's, Eukanuba and James Wellbeloved are the best. We do not advocate any semi-moist foods because of the sugar content.

PILOT'S PORRIDGE

Pilot was the name of Mr Rochester's Great Dane in *Jane Eyre*.

'burnt porridge is almost as bad as rotten potatoes:'

from *Jane Eyre*
by Charlotte Brontë

2 oz (55g) porridge oats
10 fl oz (285ml/1 $\frac{1}{4}$ cups) goats' milk/water (equal amounts of each)
$\frac{1}{2}$ apple, grated
$\frac{1}{2}$ teaspoon honey

Put the porridge oats in a saucepan and cover with goats' milk/water. Add the grated apple. Bring to the boil and simmer for five minutes, stirring all the time. Allow to cool. Drip the honey on top of Pilot's Porridge before serving.

MORNING, NOON OR NIGHT

'They gathered around the table and Dorothy ate some delicious porridge and a dish of scrambled egg and a plate of nice white bread and enjoyed her meal. Toto ate a little of everything, and was glad to get a good supper again.'

from *The Wizard of Oz*
by L. Frank Baum

2 oz (55g) Scottish porridge oats with bran
10 fl oz (285ml/1¼ cups) soy milk
1 oz (30g) soda bread, cut into small pieces
1 free range egg, scrambled

Put the porridge oats and soy milk in a saucepan. Bring to the boil, stirring all the time until most of the liquid has been absorbed. Add the soda bread and scrambled egg.

Until we read *The Wizard of Oz* it hadn't occurred to us to mix all these ingredients together, but it is delicious and a great way to start and finish the day with your dog.

BAD BREATH BISCUITS

16 oz (455g) Shipton's Irish soda coarse brown bread flour
3 oz (85g) cornmeal
3 tablespoons fresh mint, chopped
4 tablespoons fresh parsley, chopped
5 tablespoons unrefined sunflower oil
9 fl oz (255ml) natural spring water

Mix together the flour, cornmeal, mint and parsley. Add the sunflower oil and water and mix well until you have a suitable consistency for rolling out. The biscuits should be about $\frac{1}{4}$" in thickness and cut into a selection of different shapes. Bake at 350°F for 45 minutes. Allow to cool on a rack. For extra-crunchy biscuits, turn off the oven and let the biscuits dry out in the oven for five to seven hours.

Some dogs never get tartar on their teeth and these crunchy biscuits will help prevent it forming.

KEMKIBBLE

4 oz (115g) self-raising wholemeal flour
4 oz (115g) brown rice flour
1 oz (30g) organic pinhead oats
1 oz (30g) rye flakes
1 oz (30g) barley flakes
1 oz (30g) toasted oatbran
2 oz (55g) dried skimmed milk
1 tablespoon bonemeal
1 tablespoon green nori flakes
10 fl oz (285ml) water
3 tablespoons unrefined sesame oil
1 tablespoon tamari soy sauce
1 free range egg, beaten

Mix together the wholemeal flour, brown rice flour, pinhead oats, rye flakes, barley flakes, toasted oatbran, dried skimmed milk and bonemeal. Add the water. In a separate bowl combine the sesame oil, tamari soy sauce and the egg. Add this to the rest of the ingredients. Pour batter, about $\frac{1}{2}$" thick, onto a greased baking tray. Bake at 350°F for 50 minutes. Once it is cool, crumble. Put the KemKibble crumbs on a baking tray and cook in the oven at 300°F for 45 minutes. For extra-crunchy KemKibble, turn off the oven and let the kibble dry out in the oven for five to seven hours.

CREAM CAKE SLUSH

'Wilson [Elizabeth Barrett Browning's maid] did not begrudge the little dog his extra cakes and the cream from the milk (for Flush preferred milk to water) … '

from *Lady's Maid*
by Margaret Forster

2 oz banana, mashed
$\frac{1}{2}$ teaspoon honey
1 tablespoon natural yogurt
1 oz (30g) KemKibble (page 188)

Mix all the ingredients together.

STONE SOUP

In Scottish legend there is the story about Stone Soup. A weary traveller disguised as a monk accompanied by his faithful dog arrived at a remote cottage in the highlands asking the crofter for a bed for the night. He was offered a place in the barn, but what about some sustenance for him and his dog? He ventured to ask for a pot and a wee dram of water saying he would make some soup with a stone he had found on his journey. Having achieved the pot and water into which he dropped his stone, he bravely enquired if there might be an old meat bone, meekly followed by a request for a dried-up turnip. Continuing in this manner he soon had a bubbling brew of meat bone, turnip, carrots, potatoes, leeks and a pinch of salt – not forgetting the vital ingredient, the stone. This can't have been the first time 'the monk' used this method to get his supper because as soon as the crofter turned his back, he whispered to his dog, 'We mustn't forget the thyme', as he dug into his jacket pocket for their favourite seasoning.

I have found that the flavour of this soup is enhanced and goes a wee bit further if you use a stone that has a naturally formed hole in it!

16 oz (455g) meat bones
40 fl oz (2 pints UK/2 $\frac{1}{2}$ pints USA) cold water
a pinch of salt
a pinch of thyme
1 stone
1 turnip, peeled and chopped
2 carrots, sliced
1 potato, diced
1 leek, sliced

Bring the meat bones, water, salt, thyme and stone to the boil and simmer for an hour. Add the vegetables and simmer for a further 20 minutes. Allow to cool. Remove the meat from the bones. Discard the bones and the stone! Mix in the meat with the rest of the soup. You can either serve the soup as it is, or blend it to soften the meat so that it is more easily digested by an older dog.

BALTO'S BEEFED ALASKA

The bravery of Balto is legendary. In 1925 two children contracted diphtheria in the remote town of Nome in Alaska. It was vital they get medicine else they could die and the disease could spread throughout the town. However the train carrying the medicine got stuck in the snow seven hundred miles away. Balto, Gunnar's lead sled-dog, came to the rescue and against all odds managed to get the medicine to Nome in time to save the children and the town.

'Gunnar and his team pulled into town. They had made it! Balto was too tired to bark. They had been on the trail for 20 hours all together. They had driven 53 miles!'
from *The Bravest Dog Ever: The True Story of Balto*
by Natalie Standiford

6 oz (170g) beef with fat, cut into bite-sized chunks
$\frac{1}{2}$ teaspoon Bovril
4 oz (115g) brown rice, cooked in boiling water for 30–35 minutes
1 free range egg, hard-boiled and chopped

Boil the meat for 15 minutes in water flavoured with the Bovril. Strain the meat, retaining the water – 'Bovril Broth'. Mix the beef, rice and egg together. Moisten the food with some slightly warm Bovril Broth.

This is a particularly good meal for a 'working dog', being high in carbohydrates and fat which will give him the added energy he needs. The Vitamin B in Bovril will give the dog the necessary extra thiamine and riboflavin. One tablespoon of vegetable oil per pound of food could be added, to increase the fat content.

ON ALL FOURS

4 oz (115g) tripe
4 oz (115g) liver
4 oz (115g) carrots, sliced
4 oz (115g) brown rice, cooked in boiling water for 30–35 minutes

Wash the tripe and put in boiling water. Simmer for 45 minutes. Add the liver and carrots to the tripe. Simmer for a further 15 minutes. Drain. Allow to cool before chopping the tripe and liver into bite-sized portions. Mix all the ingredients with the brown rice. Made in this proportion, there is enough for a couple of meals.

Older dogs need less fat, easily digested protein and increased amounts of vitamins and minerals, so this would be an ideal meal to feed to your ageing friend.

NANA'S NURSERY NIBBLES

'As they were poor, owing to the amount of milk the children drank, this nurse was a prim Newfoundland dog, called Nana ... She believed to her last day in old-fashioned remedies like rhubarb leaf, and made sounds of contempt over all this new-fangled talk about germs, and so on.'

from *Peter Pan*
by J. M. Barrie

2–3 slices stoneground wholemeal bread made with sunflower seeds and honey, sliced and cut into cubes
Marmite, Yeast Extract, Vegemite or Vitamite

Place the bread cubes on a baking tray and cook in the oven at 300°F for 25 minutes. Put a little Marmite, Yeast Extract, Vegemite or Vitamite on each piece – your puppy will be begging for more ...

Nana's advice was good – rhubarb or rhubarb tablets are given to treat constipation. However, a word of warning: don't use rhubarb over a long period as it could prove too acidic for your dog.

SPOT'S SHUTTLE DELIGHT

'Old Mother Shuttle,
Lived in a coal-scuttle
Along with her dog and her cat;
What they ate I can't tell,
But 'tis known very well
That not one of the party was fat.'

from *Mother Shuttle*
Traditional Nursery Rhyme

4 oz (115g) lean beef, minced
2 oz (55g) swede, peeled and diced
2 oz (55g) carrots, sliced
1 free range egg, hard-boiled and chopped
1 teaspoon bonemeal

Boil the beef and vegetables in a small amount of water for 20 minutes. Drain, retaining the liquid. Add the egg and bonemeal. Moisten with liquid if desired.

This is a good diet for keeping your dog's weight under control.

BUM CHOICE

'He's a little dog, with a stubby tail,
And a moth-eaten coat of tan,
And his legs are short, of the wabbly sort;
I doubt if they ever ran;
And he howls at night, while in broad daylight
He sleeps like a bloomin' log,
And he likes the food of the gutter breed;
He's a most irregular dog.'

from *Bum*
by W. Dayton Wedgefarth

4 oz (115g) liver, chopped
1 teaspoon unrefined corn oil
2 free range eggs, beaten
1 teaspoon parsley, chopped
1 teaspoon cod liver oil
2 oz (55g) KemKibble

Fry the liver in the corn oil for six to eight minutes. Add the eggs, parsley and cod liver oil. Cook the mixture slowly, stirring occasionally until the egg has set. Mix in the KemKibble (page 188).

This is a good recipe for an older dog and should be served in small portions twice or three times a day. An older dog doesn't need as much food as a young active dog, but it's important that an older dog should have a sufficient intake of Vitamin D, calcium and phosphorus.

OF SAINT ROC & OF HIS DOG

A RHYME FOR DOG LOVERS

Good Saint Roc was a pilgrim brave,
With sandal shoon & a gourd & stave,
Good Saint Roch, as afoot I wend,
Bring me safe to my journey's end.
Good Saint Roc had a little white hound
Close at his side to leap and bound,
Little white hound, I've got one too,
Just as dear and as wise as you!
Little white hound, the roads are rife
With things that threaten a poor dog's life.
Little white hound, while mine runs free,
Keep him safe on the roads for me!
And for good Saint Roc, here's a candle round,
And a juicy bone for his little white hound!

Jessie Bayes

St Roch, also known as Roc, Rocco, and Roche lived from 1296 to 1327. He was a healer and saved many people in plague-ridden towns in southern France, Spain and Italy until sadly he caught the plague himself at Piacenza. He was expelled from the city and sought shelter in a cave where his sole companion was a dog who fetched him bread each day. Every year on St Roch's Feast Day, 16 August, Reverend Paul Jenkins, the inspiring and inventive vicar of the parish of Singleton in West Sussex, organises a Pilgrimage and open-air Service at Saint Roche's Hill, where a small chapel dedicated to St Roch existed until the mid-18th century. People flock to the service accompanied by their dogs in memory of this very special saint and his faithful dog. There the Ministry of Healing is performed.

FEAST FOR A SAINTLY HOUND

1 turnip, peeled and chopped
3 oz (85g) carrot, sliced
3 oz (85g) potato, cubed
2 oz (55g) purple sprouting broccoli spears
10 fl oz (285 ml) water
1 teaspoon bonemeal
2 oz (55g) toasted oatbran
1 oz (30g) Cheddar cheese, grated

Boil the turnip, carrot, potato and purple sprouting broccoli spears in the water for 15 minutes. Drain, saving the liquid for moistening other meals. Mix together the bonemeal, oatbran and Cheddar cheese and sprinkle on top of the vegetables.

MAX'S KEEP-FIT DIET

Henry James, the American novelist, had a Dachshund called Max. In the early 1900s when Henry James rented out his home, Lamb House, to some friends, he left a note which included the following comments regarding Max:

'The Servants, who are very fond of him [Max] and good to him, know what he 'has' and when he has it; and I shall take it kindly if he be not too often gratified with tid-bits between meals ... if he is not overfed and is sufficiently exercised, and adequately brushed ... and Burgess is allowed to occasionally wash him, I have no doubt he will remain very fit.'

from *Henry James at Home*
by H. Montgomery Hyde

6 oz (170g) raw green tripe
2 oz (55g) KemKibble (page 188)

Put the KemKibble on top of the tripe. Moisten with some luke-warm Veggie Brew (page 101) if the weather is cold.

OLD CAVALL'S DIET

King Arthur had a dog called Cavall and it is said that the dog's footprints are immortalised in stone in Wales.

4 oz (115g) chicken, beef, rabbit or venison, cooked and minced
2 oz (55g/$\frac{1}{3}$ cup) brown rice, cooked in boiling water for 30–35 minutes
1 oz (30g) carrot, grated
1 oz (30g) broccoli florets, cooked
1 free range egg, hard-boiled and chopped
Canine Care Essential Oils
Canine Care Vitamin/Mineral Supplement

Mix the meat, brown rice, carrot, broccoli florets and egg together. Just before serving, add the Canine Care Essential Oils and Canine Care Essential Vitamin/Mineral Supplement, according to the amounts specified on the packaging.

This diet is recommended for older dogs. If your pet is suffering from arthritis, Canine Care Essential Oils in his food should ease this condition.

OUT IN THE COLD

'The dog struggled feebly as she put two fingers under the green collar – there was plenty of room – and led it into the shed. As an afterthought, she threw in the ham bone it had been gnawing and some old slices of cold meat … '

from *The Plague Dogs*
by Richard Adams

1 slice of cold beef, cooked and chopped
1 slice of cold turkey, cooked and chopped
1 slice of cold chicken, cooked and chopped
1 oz (30g) cabbage leaves, shredded
1 free range egg, hard-boiled and chopped
6 oz (170g) KemKibble (page 188)

Mix all the ingredients together and moisten with some lukewarm Meaty Brew (page 62).

BULLET
BOURGIGNONNE

Bullet became well known in the 1950s as the gifted German Shepherd Dog belonging to the cowboy, Roy Rogers, and his partner Dale Evans. Bullet appeared in the film *Spoilers of the Plain* and in *The Roy Rogers Show*. At the Roy Rogers/Dale Evans Museum in California, Bullet has been preserved and can be seen together with Roy Rogers' famous horse, Trigger.

4 oz stewing steak, cubed
1 oz (30g) onion, chopped
$\frac{1}{2}$ clove garlic, crushed
$\frac{1}{4}$ teaspoon thyme, dried
1 bayleaf
5 fl oz (140ml/$\frac{1}{3}$ cup) cranberry juice

Mix all the ingredients together. Put in a casserole dish and bake in the oven at 350°F for one hour.

PIGS CAN FLY

The film *Babe* was based on Dick King-Smith's novel, *The Sheep-Pig*. Farmer Hogget's prize-winning sheep-dog, a Collie bitch called Fly teaches Babe, the little piglet won at the local fair, how to become a prize-winning sheep-pig. There were two things Fly told Babe he would have to do in order to achieve this: one was to exercise more and the other was to go on a diet.

2 free range eggs, scrambled
2 oz (55g/$\frac{1}{3}$ cup) brown rice, cooked in boiling water for 30–35 minutes
1 teaspoon bonemeal
1 teaspoon green nori flakes

Mix all the ingredients together.

OSSOBUCCO FOR A BICHON FRISÉ

'To the education of her daughters, Lady Bertram paid not the smallest attention... She was a woman who spent her days in sitting nicely dressed on a sofa, doing some long piece of needlework, of little use and no beauty, thinking more of her pug than her children ... '

from *Mansfield Park*
by Jane Austen

Barbara Taylor Bradford, the blockbuster novelist, has a Bichon Frisé called Beaji. Beaji knows too well that a writing day for the mistress of the house starts at 4.30am and finishes at 4.00pm – a slightly different life-style to Lady Bertram ...

4 oz (115g) stewing steak, cubed
1 tomato, chopped
½ clove garlic, crushed
1 tablespoon parsley, chopped
5 fl oz (140ml/¾ cup) Dashing Good Tea (page 136)
2 oz (55g) KemKibble (page 188)

Put the stewing steak, tomato, garlic and parsley in a pot filled with the Dashing Good Tea. Cover and bring to the boil. Simmer for one hour. Add KemKibble.

RECIPES FOR AILING
DOGS

'With dogs you can feed good, indifferent or bad health.'
from *The Complete Herbal Handbook for the Dog and Cat*
by Juliette de Bairacli Levy

Most dogs like garlic crushed and cooked in their food and it should help keep the fleas away as well as strengthening the digestive system. Garlic can eliminate worms and it is also recommended for dogs suffering hip pain from arthritis or dysplasia. It is said to aid in reducing blood sugar in diabetes.

> 'What does SUGAR spell?' Millicent would ask, and Hector would walk round the tea table to the sugar-bowl and lay his nose against it, gazing earnestly and clouding the silver with his moist breath.'
>
> from *Work Suspended, and Other Stories*
> by Evelyn Waugh

If your dog is suffering from diabetes, its diet should contain more protein and less fat than usual. The aim is to reduce stress on the pancreas, so one should avoid foods containing sugar. The pods of green beans contain certain hormonal substances related to insulin so they are an excellent vegetable to start adding to your dog's diet, along with Jerusalem artichokes, alfalfa sprouts and dandelion greens. With this condition it is best to feed your dog raw lean meat and some uncooked vegetables. The mineral chromium is useful for reducing blood sugar.

'If you pick up a starving dog and make him prosperous, he will not bite you. This is the principal difference between a dog and a man.'

from *Pudd'nhead Wilson*
by Mark Twain

DIET FOR DIABETES

3 oz (85g) lean beef, minced
5 oz (140g/1 cup) brown rice, cooked
1 oz (30g) mixed vegetables, chopped and uncooked (e.g. carrot, onion, parsley, alfalfa sprouts)
$\frac{1}{2}$ teaspoon brewer's yeast

OR

1 free range egg
5 oz (140g/1 cup) brown rice, cooked
1 oz (30g) mixed vegetables, chopped and cooked (Jerusalem artichokes, green beans, corn)
$\frac{1}{2}$ teaspoon dried skimmed milk

Mix all the ingredients and serve warm.

SKIN DEEP

4 oz (115g) raw lean beef, minced

2½ oz (70g/½ cup) brown rice, cooked in boiling water for 30–35 minutes

1 free range egg, hard-boiled and chopped

1 oz (30g) carrot, grated

1 tablespoon unrefined vegetable oil

a pinch of sea salt

Mix all the ingredients together and serve.

> This is a particularly good recipe for dogs suffering from skin conditions and a lacklustre coat. It is high in protein and moderate in carbohydrates and fats. The skin vitamins and minerals that can be added are Vitamin E, sulphur and zinc.

SOPHIE'S CHOICE

Sophie was the name of Alexandra's Dobermann, who died at the age of nine from a heart disease.

$2\frac{1}{2}$ oz (70g) tuna in sunflower oil, drained
OR 3 oz (85g) rabbit or venison (low in fat), cooked and diced
2 oz (55g/$\frac{1}{3}$ cup) brown rice, cooked in boiling water for 30–35 minutes
1 oz (30g) carrot, grated
$\frac{1}{2}$ teaspoon soy oil (emulsifies fats)
Canine Care Vitamin/Mineral Supplement
Canine Care Essential Oils

Mix together the tuna, rabbit or venison with the brown rice, carrot, soy oil and garlic tablet. Just before serving, add the Canine Care Essential Vitamin/Mineral Supplements and Canine Care Essential Oils, according to the amounts specified on the packaging.

WESSEX WEIGHT WATCHING DIET

'I live here: Wessex is my name;
I am a dog known rather well:
I guard the house; but how that came
To be my whim I cannot tell.'

from *A Popular Personage at Home*
by Thomas Hardy

Thomas Hardy, the English novelist, poet and dramatist, had a wire-haired Fox Terrier called Wessex (Wessie for short) who ruled the house. Wessie was insistent about listening to his favourite radio programmes, slept on the sofa and would jump on the table at mealtimes and attempt to grab the food off visitors' forks!

4 oz (115g) extra-lean beef, rabbit, venison or pigeon, cooked and cut into bite-sized pieces
1 oz (30g) carrot, grated
$\frac{1}{2}$ apple, grated
1 oz (30g) spring greens, chopped and cooked
2 oz (55g) cottage cheese
1 oz (30g) fresh egg noodles, cooked in boiling water for three to four minutes (optional)
Canine Care Vitamin/Mineral Supplement
Canine Care Antioxidant

Mix the meat, carrot, apple, spring greens, cottage cheese and egg noodles together. Just before serving, add the Canine Care Essential Vitamin/Mineral Supplements and Canine Care Anti-oxidant, according to the amounts specified on the packaging.

We recommend this diet for dogs suffering from obesity because it is low in calories and highly nutritious.

HECTOR'S HYPOALLERGENIC DIET

'A Foxhound once served me as a guide,
A good one at hill, and at valley;
    But day after day
    He led me astray,
To follow a milk-woman's tally.'

from *Lament Of A Poor Blind*
by Thomas Hood

4 oz (115g) lamb or rabbit, cooked and minced
2 oz (55g/⅓ cup) brown rice, cooked in boiling water for 30–35 minutes
Canine Care Essential Vitamin/Mineral Supplements
Canine Care Antioxidant

Mix the lamb or rabbit and brown rice together. Just before serving, add the Canine Care Essential Vitamin/Mineral Supplements and the Canine Care Anti-oxidant, according to the amounts specified on the packaging.

BOUNCE BACK BODGER

'The old dog [Bodger], barking wildly, and frantic with anxiety, for he had sensed disaster although he could not see it, waded chest deep into the churning water, but the force knocked him back again, breathless and choking; and he was forced to retreat.'

from *The Incredible Journey*
by Sheila Burnford

4 oz (115g) lean beef, minced
a pinch of salt
2 oz (55g/$\frac{1}{3}$ cup) brown rice, cooked in boiling water for 30–35 minutes
1 free range egg, hard-boiled and chopped
1 teaspoon fresh parsley, chopped
1 teaspoon wheatgerm oil

Boil the beef in a little salted water for 15 minutes. Drain, saving the liquid. Mix together the beef, rice, egg and parsley. If you can't get wheatgerm oil, crumble up a wheatgerm tablet and add to the mixture. Pour the warm liquid over the food to give it a moist, easily digested texture.

If your dog is under stress or suffering from nervous exhaustion, this meal is highly recommended.

Bachs Rescue Remedy is also excellent for a dog in a stressed condition.

CAP CANCER

One of Florence Nightingale's earliest patients was a Collie called Cap who belonged to Smither, a local shepherd. At the age of sixteen, Florence Nightingale was walking over the downs near Embley when she came across Cap suffering from a broken leg. There is no doubt that the pleasure it gave her in saving Cap, led her on to dedicating her life to caring for others.

So far nobody has been able to cap cancer, but we do know that there are certain ways of forestalling it, starting with diet. According to the North London vet, John Carter, who has done a lot of research since his own dog died of cancer, organic vegetables and fruit together with raw liver should be high on the list. Recent research also leads us to selenium as an essential trace element needed to help ward off cancer, ageing and infertility. Since the early 1970s, selenium has been added to farm animals' feed in parts of the world where natural selenium levels are low. This includes some areas of Britain, Canada and the United States.

8 oz (230g) raw liver, chopped
4 oz (115g) raw organic carrot, grated
½ oz (15g) Brazil nuts (richest natural source of selenium), ground

Mix all the ingredients and serve.

Supplement your dog's diet with selenium and Vitamins A, C and E. You can also give the herb echinacea, which is said to have anti-cancer properties.

KIDNEY KIEV

4 oz (115g) chicken, minced
½ clove garlic, crushed
1 teaspoon unrefined corn oil
3 oz (85g) brown rice, cooked in boiling water for 30–35 minutes
1 free range egg, hard-boiled and chopped
1 oz (30g) carrot, grated
½ oz (15g) apple, grated
1 teaspoon brewer's yeast

Gently fry the chicken and garlic in the corn oil. Mix with the other ingredients.

> This is a particularly good diet for a dog suffering from kidney disease. You could add to your dog's food some cod liver oil for Vitamin A as well as a Vitamin B supplement.

TAMA TORI-NO-TAKIKOMIGOHAN

A noted Japanese Chin was Tama (Japanese for 'jewel') who was owned by the Far Eastern art collector, Henri Cernuschi. Tama had the honour of being painted by both Édouard Manet and Pierre-Auguste Renoir.

1 tablespoon extra virgin olive oil
2 oz (55g) shiitake mushrooms, chopped
3 oz (85g) carrots, sliced
2 oz (55g) bean sprouts
5 fl oz (140ml) water
1 tablespoon tamari soy sauce
$\frac{1}{2}$ teaspoon honey
2 oz (55g) tofu, sliced and cubed
3 oz (85g) chicken breast, skinned and chopped into thin strips
2 oz (55g/$\frac{1}{3}$ cup) brown rice, cooked in boiling water for 30–35 minutes
1 teaspoon green nori flakes

Fry the shiitake mushrooms, carrots and bean sprouts in the olive oil for six minutes. Mix together the water, soy sauce and honey. Add the tofu, chicken and the liquid mixture to the vegetables. Cook for five minutes. Add the brown rice and green nori flakes. Bring to the boil and cook for three to four minutes, until most of the liquid has been absorbed.

This delicious Japanese dish should bring to life any dog suffering from TATT (Tired All The Time).

AROUND THE WORLD IN EIGHTEEN DOGS

'Men are generally more careful of the breed of their horses and dogs than of their children.'
from *Some Fruits of Solitude, in Reflections and Maxims relating to the conduct of Humane Life*
by William Penn

It is an interesting fact that there are more than two hundred and fifty breeds in the canine world, each one differing in their appearance and temperament. And it is not surprising to learn that the various breeds' nutritional needs vary in accordance with their geographical origins. An ideal diet for a dog in a hot country is not the same for a dog living in a cold region.

It would be impossible to deal with every breed of dog so we have taken at random various dogs, giving a brief history of their origin and *the type of food that they would have had in their natural habitat*. We are not remotely suggesting that you keep precisely to the natural foods that your dog would have eaten, but you might find it fun to trace your own dog's roots and devise a recipe for a special occasion based on the ingredients that would have been available to its ancestors.

> 'Those are Flawse hounds,' he said as one great beast leapt up and slobbered at the window with lolling tongue. 'Bred them myself from the finest stock. Two-thirds Pyrenean Mountain Dog for their ferocity and size. One-third Labrador for the keenness of scent and the ability to swim and retrieve. And finally one-third Greyhound for their speed. What do ye make of that, ma'am?'
>
> 'Four-thirds,' said Mrs Flawse, 'which is an absurdity. You can't make four-thirds of anything.'
>
> from *The Throwback*
> by Tom Sharpe

We must give due credit to William D. Cusick whose book *Canine Nutrition & Choosing The Best Food For Your Dog* inspired us to create this section in our book.

JAPANESE CHIN

The Japanese Chin was very popular with the Emperor of Japan in the 10th century and he often gave Chins as gifts to visiting dignitaries. It was Queen Alexandra who was responsible for importing the dog into England and on several occasions was painted with a Chin on her lap. The Chin's thick, lustrous coat requires optimum nutrition with a high percentage of protein in its diet to keep it in top condition. As the Chin originated near Peking their food would have been Mandarin Chinese, but later when they were bred in Japan fish featured more in their diet, along with poultry, rice and soy.

SKYE TERRIER

The defeat of the Spanish Armada in 1588 could be responsible for the origin of the Skye Terrier. It is thought that dogs shipwrecked from the Spanish fleet managed to swim ashore on the Isle of Skye where they interbred with the local terriers. However, it wasn't until the 19th century that they were called Skye Terriers. The breed became popular with Queen Victoria and Sir Edward Landseer's paintings of the royal dogs increased their popularity.

The natural food for the Skye Terrier would have been chicken, mutton and fish with a high fatty acid content. In combination with corn, wheat or potatoes this would have produced a balanced meal.

IRISH WOLFHOUND

The Irish Wolfhound arrived in Ireland during the Roman invasion. It was subsequently adopted as the Irish national dog. Its origins are found in Rome and in pre-Christian eras when it was used in battle. Its natural diet would have been high in carbohydrates and grains.

ENGLISH SETTER

The English Setter, that most elegant of gun dogs, is in fact anything but British as it was brought from Spain in the 14th century. It came from an area where wheat, corn, and game birds were plentiful and this would still be a most appropriate meal to serve an English Setter. Wheatgerm oil and safflower oil would be particularly good supplements as they require polyunsaturated fatty acids for their silky, glossy coat.

GERMAN SHEPHERD DOG

The German Shepherd Dog is also known as the Alsatian as it came from the Alsatian region of Germany. It is one of the few dogs that has the word 'dog' in its name and the first German Shepherd Dog was registered in 1899 under the name of Horand von Stephanitz. Originally they were sheep dogs and in World War I they were trained to act as messengers and locate wounded soldiers.

The German Shepherd Dog has a very short colon compared to other breeds of the same size which means a high fibre diet is essential. In Germany beef, wheat, cabbage and alfalfa would have been the normal diet.

LABRADOR RETRIEVER

The Labrador Retriever is No. 1 in the Top 10 Dog Breeds '96 registered by the Kennel Club in the UK (29,118) and the USA (120,879).

The Labrador Retriever originally came from Newfoundland in the 19th century, arriving in England on fishing boats at Poole Harbour in Dorset. Watching these dogs help the fishermen haul in their heavy nets, the locals soon adopted the Labrador Retriever as a work-mate. It showed its talents as a superb gundog and, more recently, the police world-wide use this breed as a 'sniffer' dog. And where would the blind be without this trusted friend?

The Labrador Retriever has a unique coat, being one of the few breeds able to produce an oil through the pores of its skin. However, if a Labrador Retriever is deprived in its diet of the three fatty acids in the linoleic acid group (oleic, linolenic and linoleic) then its coat will become dry and brittle, so fish oil or wheatgerm oil should be present in its diet. In Newfoundland there would have been an endless source of fish and whale fats, but in England its food would have been poultry, fish, wheat and dairy products.

ENGLISH SPRINGER SPANIEL

The English Springer Spaniel originated in Spain in the 11th century and was best known for its skill as a hunting dog of game birds. It acquired the name 'springer' for its ability to 'spring' game for the huntsmen. Its original diet would have been birds such as quail, partridge and pheasant along with corn and wheat.

GOLDEN RETRIEVER

The origin of the Golden Retriever is debatable – some sources say this breed is native to England and others say it originally came to England from Russia. However, it is agreed that the Golden Retriever as we know it today came about by the cross-breeding of yellow flat-coated dogs and Tweed Water Spaniels at Lord Tweedmouth's kennels in the 1860s.

The Golden Retriever, like the Labrador Retriever, is one of six breeds that produces oils through its skin and it is therefore essential that the correct balance of fatty acids appears in its diet. It can be assumed that the Golden Retriever's natural food would have consisted of poultry, corn and wheat.

LHASA APSO

The Lhasa Apso, originally from Tibet, was first called 'Apso Seng Kye' translated as 'Black Lion Sentinel Dogs'. They were used as 'inside' guard-dogs to the Dalai Lama – the 'outside' guarding was left to Tibetan Mastiffs. The Lhasa Apso is known for its intelligence, has always been highly honoured in its homeland and is associated with good luck. Its natural diet would have been high in carbohydrates and fibre, mainly barley and rice mixed with a bit of mountain goat, bear or llama.

If good luck is what a Lhasa Apso brings, it's not surprising to learn that Richard Burton, the famous actor, had a Lhasa Apso called 'Georgia'.

FINNISH SPITZ

The Finnish Spitz is the national dog of Finland. It is sometimes known as the 'Barking Bird Dog' because of its eager hunting skills, particularly during the grouse season. Its high-pitched bark also makes it a good guard-dog. Potatoes, oats, barley and wheat would have featured in its diet along with whale, reindeer and caribou meat.

SALUKI

Salukis were domesticated as long ago as 329 BC. The nomadic tribes in the Middle East kept this breed, exchanging it only as a gift, and it was the only dog allowed to share a sheikh's tent – any other animal was regarded as unclean. Salukis are also known as Gazelle Hounds because of their speed and ability to out-run the gazelle. Growing up in a desert environment, the saluki would have been fed on camel, rabbit, goat, brown rice, olive oil and citrus fruits. Because of the religious beliefs of their Muslim owners, Salukis would never have tasted beef or pork.

RHODESIAN RIDGEBACK

The Rhodesian Ridgeback, also known as the African Lion Hound because of its ability to hold a lion at bay, is the traditional breed of southern Africa. These dogs were bred by the European settlers for their endurance, resistance to disease and survival in extreme temperatures. The natural food for a Rhodesian Ridgeback would have been zebra, lion, elephant, gazelle, ground nuts, wheat and brown rice.

AUSTRALIAN CATTLE DOG

The Australian Cattle Dog, as the name implies, was developed in Australia for herding cattle in the outback. It wasn't until 1963 that its name was finally decided upon after a considerable amount of cross-breeding – Smithfield, Dingo, Blue Merle Highland Collie, Dalmatian, and Black and Tan Kelpie have all been mentioned in the ancestry of the Australian Cattle Dog!

The outback in Australia is not dissimilar to desert conditions, so we can assume nature's food for the Australian Cattle dog would have been oats, vegetables, kangaroo, rabbits, and beef. The diet would have been high in fibre and low in fat.

CHIHUAHAU

The Chihuahua, one of the smallest dogs in the world, is named after Chihuahua, Mexico. The Chihuahua is believed to be the result of crossing the Techichi – (a popular breed with the Toltec Indians who inhabited what we now know as Mexico in the 9th century) with a hairless breed from Asia, similar to the Chinese Crested Dog. When the Aztecs ousted the Toltecs, the Chihuahua became almost sacred to the Aztecs, who used this breed to keep the rodent population under control in the temples. Hence rodents were a good source of food together with poultry. The jungles

of Mexico would have added tropical fruits and avocados to the Chihuahua's natural diet. The Chihuahua was first seen in the USA in the 1850s but didn't reach the UK until the 1930s.

AMERICAN FOXHOUND

The American Foxhound evolved from hounds taken to the New World from England by Robert Brooke in 1650 and those imported from Ireland and France during the 18th century. They would have grown up in the south-eastern part of the USA living on raccoon, fox, squirrel, rice, corn and wheat.

BORZOI

The Borzoi, also known as the Russian Wolfhound, became almost extinct during the Russian Revolution in 1917 because the Bolsheviks took exception to this breed which was the favourite hunting dog among the aristocracy. The Borzoi hunted by sight, rather than scent. Its prey would have been wolf, rabbit and deer which formed the major part of its diet, together with alfalfa and wheat.

PEKINGESE

The Pekingese, often referred to as the Lion Dog of Peking, developed in China during the 8th century and this breed belonged solely to the Imperial family. It was considered a sacred dog and it became a capital offence to steal one. Up until 1860 when the British invaded the Imperial Palace the Pekingese had been unheard of and unseen by the rest of the world. Five dogs were captured and one was given to Queen Victoria who was instrumental in turning the Pekingese into a popular Western breed. Without doubt the original Pekes were fed well on a Mandarin diet, which would have included pork, fish, poultry, duck, greens, and rice.

WELSH CORGI

There are two types of Welsh Corgi – Cardigan and Pembroke, named after the counties from which they were bred. Both were originally used to drive cattle and referred to as 'heelers' because their method for moving stubborn animals was to nip their legs. It wasn't until 1934 that a distinction was made between the two Welsh Corgis. The Cardigan has a long tail, slightly bowed legs and rounded ears. The Pembroke is the smaller of the two, with straighter legs, pointed ears and usually has a docked tail. Their natural diets would not have been too dissimilar, mainly fish (ocean and fresh), hare, rabbit, lamb, potatoes, barley, carrots and cabbage.

WHAT'S IN

- Brush your dog's coat regularly. Check for any skin problems and examine ears, eyes, paws etc.

- Occasionally check that your dog's nails are not growing too long. If they need cutting, be careful not to cut the quick as they will bleed badly. If you have any doubts ask your vet to cut the nails for you.

- Regularly wash your dog's bed using a natural bio-degradable product and keep his covers aired. This will prevent flea eggs hatching.

- Feed your dog his food at room temperature and at the same time/s each day – preferably the main meal in the morning.

- Have fresh drinking water available at all times. Boil or filter the water for cleanliness. Change the water daily.

- Use stainless steel or ceramic dog bowls – plastic ones may affect the food or water and consequently your dog's health.

- For a truly healthy dog one hour's walk a day would not go amiss.

- Take a pooper scooper with you on walks and train your dog to use the gutter or side of paths. You can be fined if your dog fouls the footpaths or pavement.

- If your dog is wet after a walk, dry him or he may get a chill.

- When travelling in a car with a dog, make sure there is enough ventilation. Stop every hour or two to give your dog some water and exercise.

- For your dog's safety whenever he is out be sure he is wearing a collar and name-tag with your address and/or telephone number in case he should get lost.

- Do use an extension lead or a muzzle for unpredictable, eccentric dogs. I have found the best muzzles are the soft plastic ones by Roger Mugford.

- If you have a spiteful dog do consult your vet about castration as it can be helpful.

- Do try and give a home to a rescue dog. Hundreds of unwanted pets are put down every day.

- If you purchase cans of dog food, whenever possible recycle the cans. Likewise, if you buy water for your dog make sure it's in a recyclable container – (some plastic containers can have an adverse effect on health, so it is preferrable to buy water in glass bottles).

WHAT'S OUT

- Don't put your dog's bed in a damp area or where there is a draught. It is easy to make a slatted wood base to raise the bed off the floor – this also airs the bed well.

- Never overfeed your dog.

- Avoid feeding dogs the following foods: chocolate, bacon, ham, pork, parsnips and peanuts because they may cause an allergic reaction or digestive problems. Some dogs are also known to have a wheat allergy.

- Don't use added salt or sugar, white bread or white rice when cooking for your dog.

- Avoid giving an adult dog milk – he may have a lactose intolerance.

- Don't feed a dog while you are eating, despite the pleading eyes.

- Never give a complete dry food to a dog who has suffered from cystitis.

- Food should not be left down for your dog. If he has had enough or rejected it, pick it up, store it in the refrigerator, freshen it up and offer it again at room temperature. If still no joy, store it overnight, freshen it up, try again – then throw it away!

- When you are out walking don't discourage your dog from eating grasses and herbs – they are a good source of vitamins and minerals and often have a medicinal purpose; particularly couch grass (appropriately called *Agropyrum canina*) – it cleans out the intestines and can remove worms.

- Don't feed your dog for two or three hours before a car journey.

- Never leave a dog in a car without some form of ventilation, especially in hot weather. This could lead to heat stroke.

- Dogs should not be allowed to hang their heads out of a moving vehicle – something could fly into their eyes and cause injury.

- Don't leave a dog chained for long hours at a time – it can make him aggressive.

- Don't get a large dog if you are not going to walk it at least one hour a day.

In the beginning of all things, wisdom and knowledge were with the animals, for Tirawa, the One Above, did not speak directly to man. He sent certain animals to tell men that he showed himself through the beasts, and that from them, and from the stars and the sun and the moon should man learn ... all things tell of Tirawa.

Eagle Chief, Pawnee
[Letakots-Lesa] (late 19th century)
from Native American Wisdom

CONCLUSION

Until writing **Canine Care & Cuisine** with Jeannie, I was as guilty as the next person of succumbing to cheap offers and buying inexpensive dog food in bulk. However, in researching this book I started to read the small print on the tins and was startled to find that, in the majority of cases, the chicken, lamb, beef etc. advertised was a mere 4 per cent of the content while the rest was often called 'animal derivatives or animal by-products'. This effectively meant I didn't know what I was feeding my dogs.

Fortunately I had always given my dogs essential oils, vitamins and minerals which had kept them in good health with glossy coats, but I realised that nutritionally I could be doing better for them. So what did I do? I started to find a moment in my 'instant' life to begin cooking Jeannie's nutritious recipes. Sometimes if we were away I would stock up on tins of Naturediet, Pascoe's Country Dinner or Butcher's Tripe & Chicken, which all have a high meat content and itemise the contents.

I was therefore delighted when our homoeopathic vet Mark Elliott suggested that we bring out our own Canine Care products. But I suspect it's just as well he's a country vet treating pigs, sheep, cows, horses, goats etc, as I've a funny feeling that when all his dog and cat clients start to take our nutritious supplements and foods their vet bills will be down to a minimum and he won't be seeing very much of them!

Alexandra Bastedo

ALEXANDRA BASTEDO
Almodington, West Sussex

CONVERSION TABLES

Normally we don't bother to weigh the ingredients when cooking at home – we just use our own judgement. Obviously in writing a cookbook one has to be more precise, but when we came to investigate weights and measures we were driven crazy by all the slight variations in numerous cookbooks. So in the end we bought some Salter Electronic Aquatronic Kitchen Scales and laboriously weighed out all the dry and liquid ingredients and came up with the following charts. But please don't feel bound to exact weights – it's much more fun to throw in a bit of this and a bit of that once you become familiar with quantities. And the same applies to the ingredients – if you don't have a specific ingredient either leave it out or substitute with a similar food. Feel free to alter the meats (e.g. use chicken instead of lamb) and vegetables (e.g. use cauliflower instead of broccoli) in a recipe and use brown rice in place of wholemeal bread etc. Find out what your dog prefers and stick to it.

Few people in the UK use cups so the cups referred to in the recipes are USA cups.

Liquid Measurements

Imperial	Recommended ml
1 fl oz	30 ml
2 fl oz	55 ml
3 fl oz	85 ml
4 fl oz ($\frac{1}{4}$ pint USA)	115 ml
5 fl oz ($\frac{1}{4}$ pint UK)	140 ml
6 fl oz	170 ml
7 fl oz	200 ml
8 fl oz ($\frac{1}{2}$ pint USA)	230 ml
9 fl oz	255 ml
10 fl oz ($\frac{1}{2}$ pint UK)	285 ml

11 fl oz	315 ml
12 fl oz	340 ml
13 fl oz	370 ml
14 fl oz	400 ml
15 fl oz	430 ml
16 fl oz (1 pint USA)	455 ml
17 fl oz	485 ml
18 fl oz	515 ml
19 fl oz	540 ml
20 fl oz (1 pint UK)	570ml

Solid Measurements

Imperial	Recommended g
1 oz	30 g
2 oz	55 g
3 oz	85 g
4 oz ($\frac{1}{4}$ pound)	115 g
5 oz	140 g
6 oz	170 g
7 oz	200 g
8 oz ($\frac{1}{2}$ pound)	230 g
9 oz	255 g
10 oz	285 g
11 oz	315 g
12 oz ($\frac{3}{4}$ pound)	340 g
13 oz	370 g
14 oz	400 g
15 oz	430 g
16 oz (1 pound)	455 g

1 kilogram (kg) equals 2.2 lbs

USEFUL EQUIVALENTS

1.76 UK pints	= 1 litre
2 USA pints	= 1 quart
4 USA quarts	= 1 gallon
1 UK cup	= 10 fl oz
1 USA cup	= 8 fl oz

USA CUPS

1 cup bulghur wheat	= 5 oz
1 cup flour	= 4 oz
1 cup dried milk	= $2\frac{1}{4}$ oz
1 cup porridge oats	= 3 oz
1 cup raisins	= 5 oz
1 cup dried fruit	= 5 oz
1 cup rice	= 6 oz
1 cup macaroni	= 5 oz
1 cup split peas	= 8 oz
1 cup All Bran	= $2\frac{1}{4}$ oz
1 cup wheatgerm	= 3 oz
1 cup raw mince	= 7 oz

1 cup (6 oz/170g)) of uncooked brown rice yields approximately 15 oz (430g) of cooked brown rice – 2oz (55g/$\frac{1}{3}$ cup) uncooked brown rice yields 6oz of cooked brown rice

1 cup (3 oz/85g) of uncooked noodles (broken) yields approximately 6 oz (170g) of cooked noodles

1 cup (5 oz/140g) of uncooked macaroni yields approximately 12 oz (340g) cooked macaroni

1 cup (3 oz/85g) of uncooked Fusilli pasta yields approximately 8 oz (230g) cooked Fusilli

2 oz (55g) uncooked wholewheat spaghetti yields approximately 5 oz (140g) cooked wholewheat spaghetti

4 oz (115g/$\frac{3}{4}$ cup) uncooked bulghur wheat yields approximately 15 oz (430g) of soaked or cooked bulghur wheat

MEASURING SPOONS

(approximate universal conversion)

$\frac{1}{4}$ teaspoon	=	1.25 ml
$\frac{1}{2}$ teaspoon	=	2.5 ml
1 teaspoon	=	5 ml
1 tablespoon	=	15 ml

USEFUL MEASUREMENTS

3 mm	=	$\frac{1}{8}''$
6 mm	=	$\frac{1}{4}''$
1 cm	=	$\frac{1}{2}''$
2 cm	=	$\frac{3}{4}''$
2.5 cm	=	$1''$
5 cm	=	$2''$

OVEN TEMPERATURES

C	F	Gas Mark
70	150	
80	175	
100	200	
110	225	$\frac{1}{4}$
120	250	$\frac{1}{2}$
140	275	1
150	300	2
160	325	3
180	350	4
190	375	5
200	400	6
220	425	7
230	450	8
240	475	9
260	500	
270	525	
290	550	

PREFERRED PRODUCTS

AND WHERE TO FIND THEM ...

The following are products which have been recommended by dog experts and breeders:

Acorn Supplements Ltd
P O Box 103
Robertsbridge
East Sussex TN32 5ZT
Tel: 01580 881333

(Homoeopathic worming and Excel Coat plus)

Ainsworths Homoeopathic Pharmacy
36 New Cavendish Street
London W1M 7LH
Tel: 0171 935 5330
Fax: 0171 486 4313

Animal Actives
11 Southgate Road
Potters Bar
Hertfordshire EN6 5DR
Tel: 01707 646948
Fax: 01707 646948

(Natural pet products for positive pet health – slippery elm complex, canidor, euphrasia, echinacea)

Animal Fair
17 Abingdon Road
Kensington
London W8 6AH
Tel: 0171 937 0011

(One of the best pet shops in London; major stockists of most products)

Animals First
Unit 3, The Royston Centre
Lynchford Road
Ash Vale, Aldershot
Hampshire GU12 5PQ
Tel: 01252 372255
Fax: 01252 372233

(Techni-Cal Pet Food – soy free. Supported by the Canadian Veterinarian and Medical Association for its nutritional quality.)

Arden Grange International Limited
London Road
Albourne
Hassocks
East Sussex BN6 9BJ
Tel: 01273 833390
Fax: 01273 833612

(The complete dry pet food, fresh chicken is the number one ingredient – mail order)

Edward Baker Ltd
Windham Road
Sudbury
Suffolk CO10 6XD

(Bakers Complete Light [low-fat food] for dogs with a tendency to put on weight. Elite & Omega – dry dog food)

Biggles
66 Marylebone Lane
London W1M 5FF
Tel: 0171 224 5937
Fax: 0171 935 8454

(Finest special recipe sausages – 85 per cent meat, including lamb and mint, lamb and rosemary, chicken and tarragon sausages. Pork is not the best meat for dogs.)

The Bob Martin Company
Wemberham Lane, Yatton
North Somerset BS19 4BS
Tel: 01934 838061
Fax: 01934 876184

(Private family firm founded in 1892 – many excellent products including natural flea repellent collars and wormers. Main outlets: Tesco, Sainsbury's, Safeway, Asda and most pet stores.)

Bones Dog & Catalogue
The Upper Mill
Coln St Aldwyns
Cirencester
Gloucestershire GL7 5AJ
Tel: 01285 750 007
Fax: 01285 750 100

(Their catalogue includes flea patrol bandanna, flea patrol bandanna oil, non-spill water bowl, the mudlark [car seat cover], pets' picnic box, etc.)

J.L. Bragg Ltd
30 Greyfriars Road
Ipswich
Suffolk IP1 1UP
Tel: 01473 252714
Fax: 01473 288947

(Medicinal charcoal biscuits and tablets)

Burns Pet Nutrition (John Burns BVMS Lic.Ac. MRCVS)
4 Avalon Court, Kidwelly
Carmarthenshire SA17 5EJ
Tel: 01554 890482

(Real food for dogs recommended for eczema, itchy skin, ears, digestive problems, arthritis, rheumatism, heart disease, bad breath, excess moulting, unpleasant body odours and obesity.)

Butcher's Pet Care Ltd
Baker Group House, Crick
Northamptonshire NN6 7TZ
Tel: 01788 823711
Fax: 01788 825247
Sales Fax: 01788 824087

Chlorella Products Ltd
The Stables, Upper Farm
Hinton Parva, Swindon
Wiltshire SN4 0DH
Tel: 01793 791111
Fax: 01793 791122

(Chlorella, Chlorella Growth Factor, KDF/GAC Water Filter)

Comfy Pet & People Products
2–4 Parsonage Street
Bradninch, Nr. Exeter
Devon EX5 4NW
Tel: 01392 881285
Fax: 01392 881188

(Their brochure includes Waggers products, dog dri-bags, car seat protectors, plastic ventilated beds, dog food/water bowl holders, non-spill water bowls for cars and herbal flea collars.)

Denes Natural Pet Care Limited
2 Osmond Road, Hove
East Sussex BN3 1TE
Tel: 01273 325364
Fax: 01273 325704

(Denes range of complete foods and herbal medicines – ring for nearest stockist or mail order)

Dogwoode First Aid Kit for Dogs
907 Nell Gwynn House
Sloane Avenue
London SW3 3HB
Tel: 0171 584 6474
Fax: 0171 589 7503

Forbes Copper
Garston House
Sixpenny Handley
Salisbury
Wiltshire SP5 5PB
Tel: 01725 552300
Fax: 01725 552558

(Copper dog collars for rheumatism and arthritis)

Freshlands
196 Old Street
London EC1V 9FR
Tel: 0171 490 3170
Fax: 0171 490 3170

(Organic foods and natural remedies)

Fur, Feather & Fins
54 Elm Grove
Southsea
Hampshire PO5 1JG
Tel: 01705 862935
Fax: 01705 817742

(Stockists of multiple pet products)

G.S.D. Pet Foods
16 Lawrence Crescent
Dinham Road, Caerwent
Newport, Gwent NP6 4NS
Tel: 01291 421004

(100% natural dog food)

Green Ark Animal Nutrition
Unit 7B, Lineholme Mill
Burney Road, Todmorden
West Yorkshire OL14 7DH
Tel: 01706 812188
Fax: 01706 812188

(Herbal tonic, garlic powder, and many other products, including a Puppy Starter Pack and a Trial Dog Pack.)

Simon Gudgeon & Monique Woolnough
Harcourt House
West Dean, Chichester
West Sussex P018 OQY
Tel: 01243 811430

(Herbal flea collars)

Happidog Pet Foods Ltd.
Bridgend, Brownhill Lane
Longton, Preston
Lancashire PR4 4SJ
Tel: 01772 614952
Fax: 01772 614408

(The Original Vegetarian Dog Food full of vitamins and minerals)

Harrods Ltd
Pet Shop
Brompton Road, Knightsbridge
London SW1X 7XL
Tel: 0171 730 1234
Fax: 0171 581 0470

(Flea patrol bandannas, haltis and Denes pet food)

Helios Homoeopathics Ltd
89–95 Camden Road
Tunbridge Wells
Kent TN1 2QR
Tel: 01892 515111/511555
Fax: 01892 515116

(The Veterinary Homoeopathy Basic Kit plus individual range)

Hill's Pet Nutrition Ltd
1 The Beacons
Beaconsfield Road
Hatfield
Hertfordshire AL10 8EQ
Tel: 0800 282 438

(Hill's Prescription Science Diet and Hill's Science Plan – beef from Holland)

IAMS UK
Unit 2
Meadow Brook Industrial Estate
Maxwell Way, Crawley
West Sussex RH10 2SA
Tel: 01293 572100
Fax: 01293 572130

(Eukanuba dog food contains no artificial colourings, flavouring or preservatives)

Infinity Foods Co-operative Limited
67 Norway Street
Portslade
East Sussex BN41 1AE
Tel: 01273 424060
Fax: 01273 417739

(Natural and organic foods – retail outlet and wholesale suppliers)

Johnson's Veterinary Products Ltd.
5 Reddicap Trading Estate
Sutton Coldfield
West Midlands B75 7DF
Tel: 0121 378 1684
Fax: 0121 311 1758

(List of products includes Coal Tar and Sulphur Shampoo and Tea Tree Shampoo, citrus flea repellent and herbal flea collar)

Mark and Chappell Ltd.
Suite 7G, Britannia House
Leagrave Road
Luton, Beds. LU3 1RJ
Tel: 01582 405006

(Seren-um: for hyper-active and/or aggressive dogs)

Masters
14 Tews End Lane
Paulerspury
Towcester
Northants. NN12 7NQ

Tel: 01327 811758
Fax: 01327 811699

(Complete Dog Foods – Eclipse and Puppy Food. Contains meat and poultry and no by-products. Linseed is added for glossy coats.)

The Natural Dog Food Co. Ltd.
Audley Street Works
Audley Street, Mossley
Lancashire OL5 9HS
Tel: 01457 835389

(Natural wholefood diet for dogs – vegetarian contains oats, barley, maize, rye, millet, sesame seeds & selected herbs.)

Natural Friends
P O Box 103 Robertsbridge
East Sussex TN32 5ZT
Tel: 01580 881222
Fax: 01580 881444

(Suppliers of flora herbal products, Bach Flower remedies, aromatherapy oils, homoeopathic Nelsons products, homoeopathic books, pet memorials, Acorn anal clear, herbal de-wormers, flea collars & flea clear herbal capsules)

Naturediet Pet Foods Ltd
Pickhurst Road
Chiddingfold
Surrey GU8 4YD
Tel: 01428 682278
Fax: 01428 684968

(Naturediet – home delivery service – excellent moist food with top quality natural ingredients with vitamins & minerals. No added salt and it is free of artificial ingredients, colouring agents, flavour enhancers & processed meat.)

Nelson Homoeopathic Pharmacy
73 Duke Street
London W1M 5DH
Tel: 0171 629 3113

Tel: 0171 495 2404 (Mail order)
Fax: 0171 495 0013

Oscar Pet Foods
Pet, Equine & Pigeon Supplies Ltd
Bannister Hall Mill
Higher Walton, Preston
Lancashire PR5 4DB
Tel: 01772 628822
Fax: 01772 628528

(Oscar Original, Premium and Super Premium Complete Dry Dog Food-free home delivery)

Pascoe's Ltd
Dunball Wharf, Dunball
Bridgwater
Somerset TA6 4TA
Tel: 01278 425939
Fax: 01278 453503

(Their complete food is free from artificial colours, flavours and preservatives and contains vitamins, minerals & oils for a shiny coat.)

Pedigree Petfoods
Melton Mowbray
Leicestershire LE13 0BR
Tel: 01664 410000
Fax: 01664 415232

(Pedigree Veterinary Plan, Pedigree Chum Advance Formula and Pedigree Chum Puppy Food)

Pets Corner
Country Garden Centre
Bognor Road, Merston
Nr Chichester
West Sussex PO20 6EG
Tel: 01243 530606

(Stockists of multiple dog products – ring 0990 329818 for addresses of other branches in the South)

Pet Food Warehouse
Quarry Lane Industrial Estate
Chichester
West Sussex PO19 2PS
Tel: 01243 782454
Fax: 01243 531992

(Roger Mugford haltis and muzzles, Seren-um, herbal flea collars, anti-parasite shampoos)

Pet Nutrition Concepts Ltd
PO Box 201
Chichester
West Sussex PO20 7YT
Tel: 07071 223266
(Suppliers of the Canine Care Range – Essential Vitamins/Multi-Mineral, Anti-oxidant and Essential Oils.)

PETsMART
Tel: 0990 114499

(Ring for your nearest store – stockists of multiple dog products)

Pet Pavilion
Chelsea Farmers Market
125 Sydney Street
London SW3 6NR
Tel: 0171 376 8800

(Grooming, food, supplies, accessories & gifts)

Premium Pet Foods Ltd
Unit 3, Wyvern Way
Uxbridge
Middlesex UB8 2XN
Tel: 01895 810400
Fax: 01895 812397

(Nutro's Natural Choice/Nutro Max – lamb and rice preserved with Vitamin E and with linoleic acid in the form of sunflower oil – mail order.)

Pure Multi-Nutrients
8 Victory Place
Crystal Palace
London SE19 3RW
Tel: 0181 771 4522
Fax: 0181 771 4522

(Organic foods, natural remedies and macrobiotic foods – mail order)

Revital Health Shop
35 High Road
London NW10
Tel: 0181 459 3382
Fax: 0181 459 3722
Free phone: 0800 252875

(Mail order – a major stockist of various homoeopathic products and Canine Care products)

SPR
Poultry & Smallholder Centre
Greenfields Farm, Fontwell Avenue
Eastergate, West Sussex PO20 6RU
Tel: 01243 542815
Fax: 01243 544662

(Canine Care Range and animal foods)

Shipton Mill
Long Newnton
Tetbury
Gloucestershire GL8 8RP
Tel: 01666 505050
Fax: 01666 504666

(Various range of organic flours, oats etc. – mail order)

Sloane Health Shop
32 Sloane Square
London SW1W 8AQ
Tel: 0171 730 7046
Fax: 0171 823 5521

(Mail order throughout the world – various homoeopathic and biochemical remedies, Corpore Sano anti-parasite shampoo and lotion)

Specialist Pet Foods
P O Box 40 Frimley Green
Camberley
Surrey GU16 6YP
Tel: 01252 834794
Fax: 01252 834592

(Suppliers of Nutrience complete dog foods)

Spillers Petfood
P O Box 53
Newmarket
Suffolk CB8 8QF
Free phone: 0800 738 2272
Fax: 01638 552299

(Beta, Suprium, Winalot dog food and Bonios)

Stock Nutrition
Station Road, Yaxham
Norfolk NR19 1RD
Tel: 01362 694957
Fax: 01362 699067

(Genie – bio-degradable disinfectant, Protest – for digestive problems, Moor Gold – holistic tonic for older and nervous dogs and puppies, Dyna-Mite – herbal insect repellent for fleas and Dyna-Mite Shampoo. These products are also available through SPR (David Bland),Greenfields Farm, Fontwell Avenue, Eastergate, West Sussex. Tel: 01243 542815 Fax: 01243 544662)

Superdogs
1 Green View Cottages
Crambe
York YO6 7JP
Tel: 01653 618736

Plastic Bags (Pooper Scoopers)
(100 bio-degradable bags = £2.50 + 78p P&P, together with A4 sae)

Thermal Concepts Ltd.
Parc Teifi Business Park
Cardigan SA43 1EW
Tel: 01239 614005
Fax: 01239 615191

(Snuffle Safe – microwave heatpad)

Town & Country Petfoods Ltd
26 Asfordley Road
Melton Mowbray
Leicestershire LE13 OHR
Tel: 01664 63209

(Hi Life Special Care Dog Food with high meat content)

Treasurecots Pet Beds
Salters Lane
Lower Moor
Worcestershire WR10 2PE
Tel: 01386 860144
Fax: 01386 861427

(Hygienic, non-allergic, draughtproof comfortable dog beds, but not for destructive dogs who shred them when a Comfy Pet venti-lated plastic bed would be better.)

Wafcol
Haigh Avenue
South Reddish, Stockport
Cheshire SK4 1NU
Tel: 0161 480 2781
Fax: 0161 474 1896

(Specialist foods for dogs of different ages with different require-ments. Also vegetarian and hypo-allergenic. Bonemeal)

The Watermill
Little Salkeld, Penrith
Cumbria CA10 1NN
Tel: 01768 881523

(Organic dog meal and organic stoneground flours and other organic produce – family-run business with the philosophy 'care for the planet, for sustainable energy and agriculture, for the health of the soil, plants and animals...' – mail order catalogue available)

Weald & Downland Open Air Museum
Singleton, Nr Chichester
West Sussex PO18 0EU
Tel: 01243 811363
Fax: 01243 811475

(Singleton stoneground wholemeal flour)

James Wellbeloved & Co Ltd
Halfway House, Tintinhull
Nr Yeovil
Somerset BA22 8PA
Tel: 01935 825599
Fax: 01935 823280

(Quality hypo-allergenic complete dog food)

Wellington Vet Pharmacy
39 Knightsbridge
London SW1X 7NL
Tel: 0171 235 5621
Fax: 0171 235 0158

(The only veterinary pharmacy inside the M-25. They stock Nelsons & Weleda homoeopathic products – mail order throughout the world)

PARTICULAR PREFERRED PRODUCTS THAT WE USE ON OUR OWN DOGS ARE:

BEDS

Treasurecots Pet Beds – the most luxurious dogs' beds. We first found them in Harrods (at vast expense) but you can order direct (*see* Preferred Products). However, they are not suitable for chewers or diggers where plastic beds with layers of Vetbed would be more suitable.

BOWLS

Non-spill water bowls – wonderful for travelling in cars.
(*see* Comfy Pet and People Products under Preferred Products)

COMMMERCIAL DOG FOODS

Dried Food

James Wellbeloved (English), Hill's Science Plan (American), Eukanuba (American), Techni-Cal (Canadian), Nutrience (Canadian) and Pedigree Veterinary Plan are our preferred complete dried foods. However check the small print to make sure you are getting the right one for your dog's needs.

Canned/Pre-packed Food

Naturediet, Hill's Science Diet, Butcher's Tripe & Chicken, Denes and Pascoe's Country Dinner are my dogs' favourite. There may be others as good but to find out check the small print.

FLEXIS

Retractable leads. A wonderful device as a dog can still get a reasonable amount of exercise, particularly in areas that say 'keep your dog on a lead'.

HALTIS

Produced by Dr Roger Mugford. A brilliant invention. Like a horse's head collar it gives you control of the face (not the neck which is much stronger) and the piece round the muzzle tightens if the dog pulls excessively. This also gives good control over an aggressive dog.

MUZZLES

Also by Dr Roger Mugford. What dogs did before he came along I don't know. Muzzles used to be hard and scratchy. Dr Mugford's are soft plastic and much kinder to the wearer. Cloth muzzles are not so good in summer as a dog needs to sweat through its tongue and they are too confining.

SHAMPOOS

Johnson's Baby Shampoo and Coal Tar and Sulphur Shampoo

SUPPLEMENTS

Canine Care Range
Canine Care Essential Vitamins, Canine Care Essential Oils, Canine Care Multi-Mineral and Canine Care Antioxidant.

Denes
Greenleaf, garlic and seaweed.

Bob Martin
Tender Loving Care – vitamin supplement for elderly pets.

Phillips Stress
Calcium and phosphorus with Vitamins A and D.

Animal Actives
Animal Magic Royale – a liquid with Royal jelly, ginseng, damiana and capsicum.

Kai – a mixture of Western and Chinese herbs good for many chronic diseases including arthritis and eczema.

TONICS

Corpore Sano anti-parasite tonic and anti-parasite shampoo.

APPROPRIATE ADDRESSES

Agricultural and Veterinary Group of the The Royal Pharmaceutical Society of Great Britain (RPSGB)
1 Lambeth High Street
London SE1 7JN
Tel: 0171 735 9141
Fax: 0171 735 7629

Animal Aid
The Old Chapel
Bradford St
Tonbridge
Kent TN9 1AW
Tel: 01732 364546
Fax: 01732 366533

(Against all animal abuse)

Animal Aunts
45 Fairview Road
Headley Down
Hampshire GU35 8HQ
Tel: 01428 712 611
Fax: 01428 717 190
(A nationwide service providing house and animal sitters)

Animal Health Trust
P O Box 5
Newmarket
Suffolk CB8 8JH
Tel: 01638 661111
Fax: 01638 665789

Animal Medical Centre
Veterinary Treatment and Diagnostic Centre
242 Cricklewood Lane
London NW2 2PU
Tel: 0181 450 2228
Fax: 0181 208 1382

The Association of Chartered Physiotherapists in Animal Therapy (ACPAT)
Morland House
Salters Lane
Winchester
Hampshire SO22 5JP
Tel: 01962 844390

Association of Pet Behaviour Counsellors (APBC)
P O Box 46
Worcester WR8 9YS
Tel: 01386 751151
Fax: 01386 751151

Association of Pet Dog Trainers (APDT)
Peacock Farm, Northchapel
Petworth
West Sussex GU28 9JB
Tel: 01428 707620
Fax: 01428 708190

(Please send a stamped addressed envelope for your area list)

The Blue Cross
Shilton Road
Burford
Oxfordshire OX18 4PF
Tel: 01993 822651
Fax: 01993 823083

(Caring for sick animals, re-homing stray and abandoned pets)

British Association Of Homoeopathic Veterinary Surgeons
Alternative Veterinary Medicine Centre
Chinham House
Stanford-in-the-Vale
Faringdon
Oxfordshire SN7 8NQ
Tel: 01367 710324
Fax: 01367 718243

(Information and list of homoeopathetic vets)

British Homoeopathic Association
27a Devonshire Street
London W1N 1RJ
Tel: 0171 935 2163

The British Small Animal Veterinary Association (BSAVA)
Kingsley House, Church Lane
Shurdington, Cheltenham
Gloucestershire GL51 5TQ
Tel: 01242 862994

British Union for the Abolition of Vivisection (BUAV)
16a Crane Grove
London N7 8LB
Tel: 0171 700 4888
Fax: 0171 700 0252

The British Veterinary Association (BVA)
7 Mansfield Street
London W1M 0AT
Tel: 0171 636 6541
Fax: 0171 436 2970

Canine Health Census
P O Box 1, Longnor
Derbyshire SK17 0JD
(Catherine O'Driscoll)

Canine Partners for Independence (CPI)
22 Homewell
Havant
Hampshire PO9 1EE
Tel: 01705 450156
Fax: 01705 470140

Celia Hammond Animal Trust
High Street, Wadhurst
East Sussex TN5 6AG
Tel: 01892 783820/783367

Fax: 01892 784882

(Inexpensive neutering clinics and animal rescue)

Children in Hospital and Animal Therapy Association (CHATA)

87 Longland Drive, Totteridge
London N20 8HN
Tel: 0181 445 7883
Fax: 0181 445 7883

The Cinnamon Trust

Foundry House,
Foundry Square
Hayle, Cornwall TR27 4HH
Tel: 01736 757900
Fax: 01736 757010

(Helps to keep the elderly and physically weak with their pets)

Compassion in World Farming (CWF)

Charles House,
5A Charles Street
Petersfield
Hampshire GU32 3EH
Tel: 01730 264208/268863
Fax: 01730 260791

Country Fairs

Woodend
Slindon Bottom Road
Fontwell, Arundel
West Sussex BN18 OSL
Tel: 01243 544181
Mobile: 0831 430608
Fax: 01243 544068

Whightwick Mill
Bridgnorth Road
Whightwick, Wolverhampton
Staffordshire WV6 OXX
Tel: 01902 765053
Mobile: 0850 896637
Fax: 01902 765052

Dogs for the Disabled

The Old Vicarage, London Road
Ryton-on-Dunsmore
Coventry CV8 3ER
Tel: 01203 302057
Fax: 01203 302041

The Dogs' Home Battersea

4 Battersea Park Road
London SW8 4AA
Tel: 0171 622 3626
Fax: 0171 622 6451

Earth Island Institute

Earth Island Journal
300 Broadway, Suite 28
San Francisco
California 94133–3312
USA
Tel: 00 1 415 788 3666
Fax: 00 1 415 788 7324

Friends of the Earth Trust

26–28 Underwood Street
London N1 7JQ
Tel: 0171 490 1555
Fax: 0171 490 0881

Guide Dogs for the Blind Association
Hillfields
Burghfields
Reading RG7 3YG
Tel: 01734 835555
Fax: 01734 835433

Hand To Paw
North Cottage
Great Hayes
Headley Common Road
Headley
Surrey KT18 6NE
Tel: 01372 375302/0831 619847
Fax: 01372 375302
(Animal Rescue Directory)

Hearing Dogs for Deaf People
The Training Centre London
Road (A40)
Lewknor, Oxon OX9 5RY
Tel: 01844 353898
Fax: 01844 353099

The Homoeopathy Society
2 Powis Place
Great Ormond Street
London WC1N 3HT
Tel: 0171 837 9469
Fax: 0171 278 7900

Institute of Trading Standards Administration
3/5 Hadleigh Business Centre
351 London Road
Hadleigh, Essex SS7 2BT
Tel: 01702 559922
Fax: 01702 559902

The Kennel Club
1–5 Clarges Street
Piccadilly
London W1A 8AB
Tel: 0171 493 6651/629 5828
(General)
Tel: 0171 493 2001
(Registration)
Tel: 01372 743472 (Insurance)
Tel: 0171 518 1009 (Library)
Fax: 0171 518 1058
(Dog Rescue Directory/Crufts)

Meat and Livestock Commission
Snowdon Drive
Winterhill, Milton Keynes
Buckinghamshire MK6 1AX
Tel: 01908 677577
Fax: 01908 609221

Ministry of Agriculture, Fisheries and Food (MAFF)
Ergon House, c/o Nobel House
17 Smith Square
London SW1P 3JR
Tel: 0171 270 8080
Help Line: 0645 335577

Ministry of Agriculture, Fisheries and Food (MAFF)
Government Buildings (Toby Jug Site)
Hook Rise South
Tolworth
Surbiton
Surrey KT6 7NF
Tel: 0181 330 4411
Fax: 0181 337 3640
(List of quarantine kennels)

National Animal Welfare Trust (NAWT)
Tyler's Way
Watford by-Pass
Watford
Hertfordshire WD2 8HQ
Tel: 0181 950 8215/0177

The National Anti-Vivisection Society Limited
261 Goldhawk Road
London W12 9PE
Tel: 0181 846 9777
Fax: 0181 846 9712

(Animal Defenders, The Lord Dowding Fund for Humane Research)

National Canine Defence League (NCDL)
17 Wakley Street
London EC1V 7LT
Tel: 0171 837 0006
Fax: 0171 833 2701

(NCDL's rescue centres)

National Office of Animal Health Limited (NOAH)
3 Crossfield Chambers
Gladbeck Way
Enfield
Middlesex EN2 7HF
Tel: 0181 367 3131
Fax: 0181 363 1155

The National Pet Register
Thorpe Underwood Hall
York Y05 9SZ
Tel: 0700 0800 123

(Computerised tracing for lost dogs – registration and insurance)

National Pet Week
P O Box 101
Northwood
Middlesex HA6 3RH
Tel: 0181 428 7369
Fax: 0181 428 7369

(People for Pets – Pets for People)

Passports for Pets
20 Seymour Road
London SW18 5JA
Tel: 0181 870 5960
Fax: 0181 870 9223
(The alternative to quarantine)

People for the Ethical Treatment of Animals (PETA)
P O Box 3169
London NW1 2JF
Tel: 0181 785 3113

People's Dispensary For Sick Animals (PDSA)
Whitechapel Way
Priorslee
Telford
Shropshire TF2 9PQ
Tel: 01952 290999
Fax: 01952 291035

Pet Care Trust
Bedford Business Centre
170 Mile Road
Bedford MK42 9YZ

Tel: 01234 273933
Fax: 01234 273550

The Pet Food Manufacturers' Association (PFMA)

Suite 1/2 12–13 Henrietta Street
London WC2E 8LH
Tel: 0171 379 9009
Fax: 0171 379 8008/3898

Pet Health Council

Thistledown Cottage
49 Main Street
Sewstern
Grantham
Lincolnshire NG33 5RF
Tel: 01476 861379
Fax: 01476 861336

Promoting The Value Of Dogs For The Benefit Of People & Pets As Therapy (PRO DOGS & PAT DOGS)

Rocky Bank, 4–6 New Road
Ditton, Aylesford, Maidstone
Kent   ME20 6AD
Tel: 01732 872222/848499

The Protesters Animal Information Network Limited (P.A.I.N.)

The Lodge
Broadhurst Manor
Horsted Keynes
West Sussex   RH17 7BG
Tel: 01342 811377
Fax: 01342 811213

(Carla Lane and Celia Hammond. Carla Lane has also set up Animal Line and Animal Rescue.)

Raystede Centre for Animal Welfare Limited

Raystede, Ringmer
East Sussex BN8 5AJ
Tel: 01825 840252

Royal College of Veterinary Surgeons

Belgravia House
62–64 Horseferry Road
London SW1P 2AF
Tel: 0171 222 2001
Fax: 0171 222 2004

Royal Society for the Prevention of Cruelty to Animals – (RSPCA)

Causeway
Horsham
West Sussex RH12 1HG
Tel: 01403 264181
Fax: 01403 241048
Cruelty Line: 0990 555999

Royal Veterinary College

Camden Campus
Royal College Street
London NW1 OTU
Tel: 0171 468 5000
Fax: 0171 388 2342
(The Beaumont Animals' Hospital Tel: 0171 387 8134)

Hawkshead Campus
Hawkshead Lane,
North Mimms
Hatfield, Herts. AL9 7TA

Tel: 01707 666333
Fax: 01707 652090
(ACT – Animal Care Trust)

The Scottish Kennel Club
3 Brunswick Place
Edinburgh EH7 5HP
Tel: 0131 557 2877
Fax: 0131 556 6784

Scottish Society for the Prevention of Cruelty to Animals (SPCA)
Braehead Mains, 603
Queensferry Road
Edinburgh EH4 6EA
Tel: 0131 339 0222
Fax: 0131 339 4777

Society for Companion Animal Studies (SCAS)
10b Leny Road
Callander
Scotland FK17 8BA
Tel: 01877 330996
Fax: 01877 330996

(Includes Pet Loss Advisory Group)

Soil Association
86 Colston Street
Bristol BS1 5BB
Tel: 0117 929 0661
Fax: 0117 925 2504

(Directory of organic farm shops and box schemes)

Support Dogs
P O Box 447
Sheffield S6 6YZ
Tel: 0114 232 0026
Fax: 0114 232 0026

Therapaws
The Canine Therapeutic and Leisure Swimming Pool
Street End Lane
Sidlesham, Chichester
West Sussex PO20 7RG
Tel: 01243 641114

Ulster Society for the Prevention of Cruelty to Animals (USPCA)
Unit 4, Boucher Business Centre
Apollo Road, Belfast   BT12 6HP
Tel: 01232 660479
Fax: 01232 381911
Animal Helpline: 0990 134329

Vegan Society
Donald Watson House
7 Battle Road
St Leonards-on-Sea
East Sussex TN37 7AA
Tel: 01424 427393
Fax: 01424 717064

Vegetarian Society
Parkdale
Dunham Road
Altrincham
Cheshire WA14 4QG
Tel: 0161 928 0793
Fax: 0161 926 9182

Which?
P O Box 44
Hertford X SG14 1SH
Tel: 01992 822800
Fax: 0171 830 8585

World Society for the Protection of Animals
2 Langley Lane
London SW8 1TJ
Tel: 0171 793 0540
Fax: 0171 793 0208

NOTABLE NAMES

Mr Trevor Adams BVSc CertBR VetMFHom MRCVS
The Orchard Veterinary Surgery,
King Street, Glastonbury
Somerset BA6 9JX
Tel: 01458 832972

(Homoeopathic vet)

Mr Richard Allport BVetMed VetMFHom MRCVS
Natural Medicine Veterinary Centre
11 Southgate Road, Potters Bar
Hertfordshire EN6 5DR
Tel: 01701 662058
Fax: 01701 646948

(Referral service in: acupuncture, Bach flower therapy, electro crystal therapy, homoeopathy, healing, herbal medicine, aromatherapy, physiotherapy, massage, osteopathy and behaviour counselling and promotes a large range of natural products.) See Animal Actives in Preferred Products.

Dr Ian Billinghurst
P O Box 703
Lithgow
New South Wales 2790
Australia

(Noted Australian vet, author of *Give Your Dog A Bone.*)

Katie Boyle
c\o J. Gurnett Ltd
2 New Kings Road
London SW6 4SA
Tel: 0171 736 7828

(Author of *Battersea Tails*, Agony Aunt on *Dogs Today*, on the Committee of Management of The Dogs' Home Battersea for over twenty years, Patron of National Canine Defence League, Animal Health Trust & Animal Welfare Trust)

Mr Keith Butt MA VetMB MRCVS
8 Kynance Mews
Gloucester Road
London SW7 4QP
Tel: 0171 584 2019

(A London general vet who was brilliant with Blue, my Dobermann who had hip dysplasia. His particular interests are skin and cancer.)

Mr John Carter BVetMed MRCVS
290 Kenton Road
Harrow
Middlesex HA3 8DD
Tel: 0181 907 6051

(Specialises in cancer and leukaemia. Good success rates.)

Mr Timothy Couzens BVetMed VetMFHom MRCVS
Holistic Veterinary Medicine Centre
The Village Works, London Road
East Hoathly, Lewes
East Sussex BN8 6QA
Tel: 01825 840966

(Homoeopathic vet)

Mr Christopher Day MA VetMB VetMFHom MRCVS
Alternative Veterinary Medicine Centre
Chinham House, Stanford-in-the-Vale
Faringdon
Oxfordshire SN7 8NQ
Tel: 01367 710324

(Homoeopathic vet.)

Juliette de Bairacli Levy
(Extremely knowledgeable on herbs and homoeopathy and nutrition for different dogs. Author of *The Complete Herbal Handbook For the Dog and Cat*.)

Dr Ian Dunbar BVetMed BSc PhD
Center for Applied Animal Behaviour
2140 Shattuck Avenue #2406
Berkeley, California 94704
USA
Tel: 00 1 510 658 8588

(The television vet – *Dogs With Dunbar* – and expert on dog behaviour)

Mr Mark Elliott BVSc VetMFHom MRCVS
Kingley Veterinary Centre
Oldwick Farm, West Stoke Road
Lavant, Nr Chichester
West Sussex PO18 9AA
Tel: 01243 528899
Fax: 01243 528877

(Our homoeopathic/acupuncturist vet and adviser.)

Dr Bruce Fogle DVM(Gu) MRCVS
86 York Street
London W1H 1DP
Tel: 0171 723 2068

(Excellent vet, journalist and author of superb dog books including *First Aid for Dogs*, *101 Essential Tips Caring for Your Dog*, *The Dog Encyclopedia*.)

Mr Peter Graham Goodrich BVetMed VetMFHom MRCVS

Kingston House
85 Main Street
Pembroke, Dyfed SA71 4DB
Tel: 01646 622943

(Homoeopathic vet)

Mr Peter Gregory BVSc VetMFHom MRCVS

6 Queen Street
Newcastle under Lyme
Staffordshire ST5 1ED
Tel: 01782 719771

(Homoeopathic vet)

Celia Hammond

High Street, Wadhurst
East Sussex TN5 6AG
Tel: 01892 783820/783367
Fax: 01892 784882

(Founder of inexpensive neutering and spaying clinics for dogs and cats)

Mr John Hoare BVSc VetMFHom MRCVS

12 Martins Road
Hanham, Bristol
Avon BS15 3EW
Tel: 0117 967 7067

(Homoeopathic vet)

Mr Francis Hunter VetMFHom MRCVS

Arun Veterinary Group
121 Lower Street
Pulborough
West Sussex RH20 2BP
Tel: 01798 872089

(Homoeopathic vet – Chairman of the British Homoeopathic Association. a charity whose aim is to promote homoeopathy for people and animals; former president of the British Association of Homoeopathic Veterinary Surgeons.)

Mrs Barbara Jones BVMS VetMFHom MRCVS
Oakwood Veterinary Centre
Babbinswood Farm
Whittington, Oswestry
Shropshire SY11 4PH
Tel: 01691 679699

(Homoeopathic vet and canine acupuncturist)

Mr Richard Lockyer BVMS VetMFHom MRCVS
Highfield Veterinary Surgery
White Stubbs Lane
Broxbourne
Hertfordshire EN10 7QA
Tel: 01992 440738

(Homoeopathic vet)

Mr Tom Lonsdale BVetMed MRCVS
Riverstone Veterinary Hospital
Garfield Road
Riverstone
New South Wales 2765
Australia

Catherine O'Driscoll
PO Box 1, Longnor
Derbyshire SK17 0JD

(Instigator of the Canine Health Census, author of *The Darling Buds of May* which is about vaccinations, runs Abbeywood Publishing Ltd. – please send s.a.e. for details)

Dr Richard H Pitcairn, D.V.M., Ph.D.
Director
1283 Lincoln Street
Eugene, Oregon 97401
USA
Tel: 00 1 503 342 7665

(Co-author of *Dr Pitcairn's Complete Guide to Natural Health for Dogs and Cats.*)

Mr John Saxton BVetMed VetMFHom MRCVS
Tower Wood Veterinary Group
27 Tinshill Road
Leeds LS16 7DR
Tel: 01132 678419

(Homoeopathic vet)

Miss Christine Shields BVSc VetMFHom MRCVS
43 Main Street,
Warton, Carnforth
Lancashire LA5 9NT
Tel: 01524 736765

(Homoeopathic vet)

William George Smith
29 Elm Road
Westergate, Chichester
West Sussex P020 6RQ
Tel: 01243 543991

(Spiritual healer)

Mrs June Third-Carter BVMS VetMFHom MRCVS
Hillhead House
Lonmay, By Fraserburgh
Aberdeenshire AB43 4UP
Tel: 01346 532948

(Homoeopathic vet)

Mrs Susan Thomas MA VetMB VetMFHom MRCVS
Tower Wood Veterinary Group
27 Tinshill Road
Leeds   LS16 7DR
Tel: 01132 678419
(Homoeopathic vet)

'BELIEVE IT OR NOT!' – THE BIBLIOGRAPHY

Dr. Pitcairn's Complete Guide to Natural Health for Dogs & Cats
Richard H. Pitcairn, D.V.M., Ph.D., and
Susan Hubble Pitcairn
Rodale Press, Inc., 1995

101 Essential Tips Caring for your Dog
Dr. Bruce Fogle DVM, MRCVS
Dorling Kindersley Publishers Limited, 1995

You & Your Dog
The Complete Owner's Guide to Dogs:
Their Care, Health And Behaviour
David Taylor B.V.M.S. F.R.C.V.S. with Peter Scott M.R.C.V.S.
Dorling Kindersley Publishers Limited, 1994

In Accord With Nature
A Comprehensive Guide to Giving Your Dog A Healthy Lifestyle
Denes Natural Pet Care Limited

The Natural Remedy Book for Dogs & Cats
Diane Stein
The Crossing Press, 1994

Clinical Nutrition of the Dog and Cat
JW Simpson, RS Anderson, PJ Markwell
Blackwell Scientific Publications, 1993

The Dog
The Complete Guide To Dogs And Their World
David Alderton
Quill Publishing Limited, 1987

Canine Nutrition & Choosing The Best Food For Your Breed of Dog
William D. Cusick
Adele Publications, Inc., 1990

How to care for your older dog
Bill Landesman & Kathleen Berman
New English Library, 1978

Who Killed the Darling Buds of May?
1: Vaccination – What Vets Don't Tell You About Vaccines
Catherine O'Driscoll
Abbeywood Publishing (Vaccines) Ltd., 1997

Give Your Dog A Bone
Dr Ian Billinghurst
available in the UK from Abbeywood Publishing Ltd.

The Doctors Book of Home Remedies for Dogs and Cats
By the Editors of *Prevention* Magazine Health Books
Edited by Matthew Hoffman
Rodale Press, Inc., 1996

Natural Healing for Dogs & Cats
Diane Stein
The Crossing Press, 1993

Natural Health, Natural Medicine
Andrew Weil, M.D.
Warner Books, 1997

Dogs: Homoeopathic Remedies
George Macleod, MRCVS, DVSM
The C.W. Daniel Co. Ltd.

Dogs and Homoeopathy, The Owner's Companion
Mark Elliott BVSc VetMFHom MRCVS & Tony Pinkus BPharm. MRPharmsS
Ainsworths Homoeopathic Pharmacy, 1996

Do Dogs Need Shrinks?
Dr Peter Neville
Pan Books Limited, 1993

Dogs Never Lie About Love
Reflections on the Emotional World of Dogs
Jeffrey Masson
Jonathan Cape, 1997

You Don't Have To Feel Unwell!
Nutrition, Lifestyle, Herbs and Homeopathy
Robin Needes
Gateway Books, 1994

The Practically Macrobiotic Cookbook
Preparation of more than 200 delicious recipes
Keith Michell
Thorsons Publishing Group, 1987
(a new, revised edition is planned to be published in 1998 by Inner Traditions, 1 Park St., Rochester, Vermont 05767, USA)

About Macrobiotics
The Way of Eating
Craig Sams
Thorsons Publishers Limited,
1983

The Vegan Cookbook
Alan Wakeman and Gordon
Baskerville
Faber and Faber, 1996

**Friends of the Earth
Cookbook**
Veronica Sekules
Penguin Books, 1981

The Kind Food Guide
Audrey Eyton
Penguin Books

**BSE: The Facts
Mad Cow Disease and the
Risk to Mankind**
Brian J. Ford
Corgi Books, 1996

**The Literary Companion to
Dogs**
Christopher Hawtree
Sinclair-Stevenson, 1993

Lady's Maid
Margaret Forster
Chatto & Windus Limited,
1990

Jane Eyre
Charlotte Brontë
Thomas Nelson and Sons Ltd

The Wizard of Oz
L. Frank Baum
Puffin Books, 1982 [original
1900]

**The Hundred and One
Dalmatians**
Dodie Smith
Mammoth, 1996 [original
1956]

The Starlight Barking
Dodie Smith
Puffin Books, 1970

Space Dog the Hero
Natalie Standiford
Hutchinson, 1991

Peter Pan
J.M. Barrie
Everyman's Library Children's
Classics, 1992
[original 1911]

**Mother Goose's Nursery
Rhymes**
edited by L. Edna Walter
Adam and Charles Black, 1951
[original 1924]

Dictionary of Quotations
Bloomsbury Publishing
Limited, 1987

**Brewer's Dictionary of Phrase
and Fable**
Ivor H. Evans
Cassell Publishers Ltd., 1988

Dogs
Armard Eisen
Ariel Books, 1992

The Pickwick Papers
Charles Dickens
Penguin Books Ltd., 1986
[original 1836]

Faithful to the End
The Daily Telegraph
Anthology of Dogs
Celia Haddon
Headline Book Publishing PLC,
1991

Kipper's Birthday
Mick Inkpen
Hodder Children's Books, 1993

**Dr Xargle's Book of Earth
Hounds**
Jeanne Willis and Tony Ross
Random Century Children's
Books, 1989

Babe – The Sheep-Pig
Dick King-Smith
Puffin Books, 1985

**The Call of the Wild, White
Fang, and Other Stories**
Jack London
Penguin Books, 1993

**The Bravest Dog Ever
The True Story of Balto**
Natalie Standiford
Red Fox, 1996

Aesop's Fables
Retold by Jacqueline Morley
Macdonald Young Books, 1995

Travels with Charley
John Steinbeck
Mandarin (first published by
William Heinemann in 1962)

Lady With Lapdog
Anton Chekhov
Penguin Books, 1964

**The Complete Nonsense of
Edward Lear**
edited and introduced by
Holbrook Jackson
Faber and Faber Limited

Footfalls in Memory
Terry Waite
Coronet Books, 1995

Just So Stories
Rudyard Kipling
Penguin Books, 1994 [first published 1902]

Les Chiens de Paris
Barnaby Conrad III
Thames & Hudson Ltd., 1995

The Cherry Orchard
Anton Chekhov
Faber and Faber, 1989 [first published 1978]

Ingrid Bergman My Story
Ingrid Bergman and Alan Burgess
Sphere Books Ltd., 1981

The Poetical Works of Rupert Brooke
Edited by Geoffrey Keynes
Faber and Faber, 1970 [first published 1946]

Five Go Adventuring Again
Enid Blyton
Hodder Children's Books, 1995 [first published 1942]

The Plague Dogs
Richard Adams
Penguin Books Ltd, 1982 [first published 1977]

Dumb Witness
Agatha Christie
HarperCollins Publishers, 1994 [first published 1937]

Of Mice and Men
John Steinbeck
Minerva, 1995 [first published 1937]

Black Dogs
Ian McEwan
Picador, 1993 [first published 1992]

The Hound of the Baskervilles
Conan Doyle
Oxford University Press, 1993

Far From The Madding Crowd
Thomas Hardy
Mammoth [first published 1874]

Mansfield Park
Jane Austen
Penguin Books, 1985 [first published 1814]

Rebecca
Daphne Du Maurier
Arrow, 1997 [first published 1938]

Sussex Seams - A Collection of Travel Writing
Edited by Paul Foster
Alan Sutton Publishing Ltd., 1996

Spot Bakes a Cake
Eric Hill
Puffin, 1996 [first published 1994]

The Dog In Art From Rococo To Post Modernism
Robert Rosenblum
John Murray (Publishers) Ltd., 1988

100 Favourite Animal Poems
chosen by Laurence Cotterell
Judy Piatkus (Publishers) Ltd., 1992

Animal Verse
compiled by Raymond Wilson
Beaver Books, 1982

The Penguin Book of Animal Verse
Introduced and edited by George MacBeth
Penguin Books Ltd., 1965

Plague and Fire: London 1665–66
Leonard W. Cowie
Wayland (Publishers) Ltd, 1970

The New English Bible – New Testament
Oxford University Press
Cambridge University Press, 1961

Native American Wisdom
Running Press Book Publishers

Heal Your Dog The Natural Way
Richard Allport BVetMed VetMFHom MRCVS
Mitchell Beazley, 1997

The Complete Book of Dog Care
Tim Hawcroft BVSc(Hons), MACVSc, MRCVS
Ringpress Books Limited, 1992

Immune for Life
Live Longer and Better by Strengthening Your 'Doctor Within'
Arnold Fox, M.D. & Barry Fox, Ph.D.
Prima Publishing, 1990

The Complete Works of Saki
The Bodley Head Ltd, 1989

Shirley
Charlotte Brontë
Penguin Books, 1985

The Voyage of a Naturalist
Charles Darwin, autobiographical writings selected and arranged by Christopher Ralling
BBC, 1978

David Copperfield
Charles Dickens
Oxford University Press, 1991

Three Men in a Boat
Jerome K Jerome
Pavilion Books Ltd, 1989

The Tale of Ginger and Pickles
Beatrix Potter
F Warne & Co Ltd,

Fables For Our Time
James Thurber
Harper & Row, 1940

The Definitive Edition of Rudyard Kipling's Verse
Hodder and Stoughton, 1986 [first published 1940]

Auguries of Innocence
William Blake
Flansham Press, 1914

George Orwell
Michael Shelden
William Heinemann, 1991

The Incredible Journey
Sheila Burnford
Hodder Children's Books, 1995
[first published 1961]

A Classic Illustrated Treasury
– Dogs
Pavillion Books, 1992

So late into the Night,
Byron's Letters and Journals
edited by Leslie A. Marchand
Volume 5 1816–1817 John
Murray Publishers Ltd., 1976

The Letters of Elizabeth
Barrett Browning to Mary
Russell Mitford
Edited by Meredith B. Raymond
and Mary Rose Sullivan
Armstrong Browning Library of
Baylor University
1983

Oliver Twist
Charles Dickens
Oxford University Press

Exemplary Novels
Miguel de Cervantes
Aris & Phillips, 1992

The Complete Poems
Thomas Hardy
ed. James Gibson
Papermac, 1976

Life of Patrick White
David Marr
Jonathan Cape, 1991

Letters of a Lifetime
ed Jerrold Northrop Moore
Oxford University Press, 1990

The Story of My Life
Ellen Terry
Hutchinson, 1988

The Throwback
Tom Sharpe
Pan Books, 1980

Henry James at Home
H Montgomery Hyde
Methuen, 1969

Work Suspended & Other
Stories
Evelyn Waugh
Penguin Books Ltd, 1997

More Leaves from the Journal
of a Life in the Highlands
Queen Victoria
Smith Elder, 1884

The Life of Florence
Nightingale,
Vol. 1 (1820–1861)
Sir Edward Cook
Macmillan and Co. Limited,
1914

LITERARY ACKNOWLEDGEMENTS

Acknowledgement and thanks are due to the following for kindly giving us permission to reproduce or make reference to copyright material:

Extract from *Dr Xargle's Book of Earth Hounds* by Jeanne Willis and Tony Ross, published by Anderson Press Ltd., London. © Text Jeanne Willis 1989.

Richard Allport BVetMed VetMFHom MRCVS: references to material in his leaflet 'Animal Actives' and his book *Heal Your Dog the Natural Way*.

Amanda Barton-Chapple: poem 'What I Love About My Dog Tippy' from *Never, Grandma, Never*.

Extract from *Five Go Adventuring Again*. Text copyright © Enid Blyton Ltd. Published by Hodder Children's Books.

Agatha Christie Ltd and Hughes Massie Ltd.: extract from *Dumb Witness* by Agatha Christie, published by HarperCollins. © Agatha Christie, Mallowan 1937.

Timothy Couzens BVetMed VetMFHom MRCVS: reference to his article 'Controlling Fleas' in the magazine *Pet Dogs*, April 1997.

Extract from *Henry James at Home* by H. Montgomery Hyde. Copyright H. Montgomery Hyde, reproduced by permission of Curtis Brown Group Ltd, London.

quote from 'News From Hill's' from *Dogs for the Disabled Newsletter*, Issue 19, October 1996.

Two extracts from *The Incredible Journey* by Sheila Burnford reproduced by permission of Hodder and Stoughton Limited. Copyright © 1960 Sheila Burnford.

Extract from *Kipper's Birthday* by Mick Inkpen, reproduced by permission of Hodder and Stoughton Limited. Text and illustrations copyright © Mick Inkpen.

Francis Hunter VetMFHom MRCVS: information on worming and his homoeopathic remedy for diabetes.

The Revd Paul Jenkins MA BEd: Poem 'Of Saint Roc and of His Dog: A Rhyme for Dog Lovers' by Jessie Bayes from *The Pilgrim* – the annual newsletter of the Fraternity of Saint Roch, No. 1, 1996.

Macmillan: extract from the poem 'A Popular Personage at Home' from *The Complete Poems* by Thomas Hardy, ed. James Gibson, published by Papermac, 1976; extract from *Far From the Madding Crowd* by Thomas Hardy, published by Papermac, 1976.

Keith Michell: extracts from *The Practically Macrobiotic Cookbook*, published by Thorsons Publishing Group. © Keith Michell 1987.

John Murray (Publishers) Ltd.: extract from *The Letters of Elizabeth Barrett Browning to Mary Russell Mitford 1836–54* (volume II) edited and introduced by Meredith B. Raymond and Mary Rose Sullivan. Copyright © Browning Letters, John Murray, 1983; extract from Lord Byron's letter to John Cam Hobhouse, 19 December, 1816, from *'So Late into the Night' Byron's Letters and Journals* (volume 5, 1816–17) edited by Leslie A. Marchand; extract from *The Hound of the Baskervilles* by Arthur Conan Doyle.

Catherine O'Driscoll: reference to material in her book, *Who Killed the Darling Buds of May? – What Vets Don't Tell You About Vaccines*, published by Abbeywood Publishing (Vaccines) Ltd, 1997.

Extract from *Edward Elgar: Letters of a Lifetime* ed. Jerrold Northrop Moore (Oxford University Press 1990). Reprinted by permission of Oxford University Press.

Laurence Pollinger Ltd. on behalf of Viking Penguin Inc.: extract from *Small Beer – 'Dog Story'* by Ludwig Bemelmans, published by John Lane, The Bodley Head.

Random House UK Limited: extract from *Space Dog the Hero* by Natalie Standiford, published by Hutchinson Children's Books; extract from *Travels with Charley* by John Steinbeck, published by William Heinemann; copyright © 1962 by John Steinbeck. Extract from *Of Mice and Men* by John Steinbeck, published by William Heinemann. Copyright © 1937 by John Steinbeck; extract from *George Orwell* by Michael Shelden, published by Minerva; extracts from *Lady's Maid* by Margaret Forster, published by Chatto & Windus. Copyright © Margaret Forster 1990; extract from *The Bravest Dog Ever/The True Story of Balto* by Natalie Standiford, published by Red Fox. Copyright © Text Natalie Standiford 1989; extract from *The Throwback* by Tom Sharpe, published by Secker & Warburg.

Running Press Book Publishers: two quotations by Mourning Dove and Eagle Chief reprinted with permission from *Native American Wisdom*, copyright © 1993 by Running Press.

Gar Smith, editor of *Earth Island Journal* (San Francisco, California USA): reference to the articles 'The Truth About Cats and Dogs' by Ann Martin and 'Food Not Fit For a Pet' by Dr Wendell O. Belfield DVM, which appeared in *Earth Island Journal* volume 11, number 3, summer 1996; *The Dark Side of Recycling,* Fall 1990.

The Society of Authors as the literary representative of the Estate of Virginia Woolf: extract from *On a Faithful Friend* by Virginia Woolf, the *Guardian*, 18 January 1905.

A.P. Watt Ltd on behalf of The National Trust: extract from the poem 'The Power of the Dog' by Rudyard Kipling from *The Definitive Edition of Rudyard Kipling's Verse*, published by Hodder and Stoughton.

A.P. Watt Ltd on behalf of The Society ot Authors: extract from *Three Men In a Boat* by Jerome K Jerome, published by Pavilion Books Ltd.

Every reasonable care has been taken to trace ownership of copyrighted material. Information that will enable the publishers to rectify any reference or credit is welcome.

I pray you who own me, let me continue to live close to Nature. Know that: I love to run beneath the sun, the moon and the stars; I need to feel the storm winds around me, and the touch of rain, hail, sleet and snow; I need to splash in streams and brooks, and to swim in ponds, lakes, rivers and seas; I need to be allowed to retain my kinship with Nature.

Juliette de Bairacli Levy
from *The Complete Herbal Handbook for the Dog and Cat*

'Stop running those dogs on your page. I wouldn't have them peeing on my cheapest rug.'

William Randolph Hearst
From *Dictionary of Quotations*

(referring to the publication of James Thurber's drawings by one of his editors.)

THE END